Bluffer's®

GUIDE TO

MANAGEMENT

EDITED BY JOHN WINTERSON RICHARDS

© Haynes Publishing 2018
Published June 2018

With kind acknowledgements to John Courtis and
Elizabeth B Ratcliffe, authors of earlier editions of
The Bluffer's Guide to Management

Additional contributions by Andy Stevens.

A CIP Catalogue record for this book
is available from the British Library.

ISBN: 978 1 78521 225 3

Library of Congress control no. 2018932888

Published by Haynes Publishing,
Sparkford, Yeovil, Somerset BA22 7JJ
Tel: 01963 440635
Int. tel: +44 1963 440635
Website: www.haynes.com

Printed in Malaysia.

Series Editor: David Allsop.
Front cover illustration by Alan Capel.

CONTENTS

The perfect manager seeks to rise above the herd while, at the same time, appearing to desire nothing more than to remain part of it.

THE SECRET
OF MANAGEMENT

The great secret of management is that it is actually rather easy. This is a secret because if everyone knew how easy it was, everyone – all right, nearly everyone – could probably do it. Then what would be the point of having managers?

Worse, what would be the point of being a manager? To whom would the prestige and the status be accorded? What would happen to the extra money and the perks? They might go to the people who can actually do things rather than to the people who tell them to do them. The horror!

So the role of bluffing in management is not only about pretending to be more knowledgeable than you are. It is also about pretending that it is necessary to be more knowledgeable than you are.

Most of the academic discipline of 'management science' consists of making things that are in themselves rather simple appear complex. Indeed, the whole process begins by calling it a 'science'. There is nothing particularly scientific about management. It is, like bluffing itself, more of an art.

Like any art, it depends on the mastery of a few basics, but those basics can be summarised in a short book…about this size, as it happens.

Management poses as a big subject with lots of different aspects. The word management can be used as a prefix to form a broad range of threatening terms – management techniques, theories, functions, tools, and so on and so on. How can you hope to understand them all? Fortunately you do not have to.

The essence of bluffing is to retain control of a situation, or at least your position in it, without enough data, assets, ability or power to justify that retention. That, as it happens, is also the essence of most management.

In some ways management should need no introduction. We are all exposed to it on a daily basis, and not just at work. Daily survival in the 21st century depends on smooth management. Most of the glitches you face in your daily life, from compromising emails sent to the wrong person to not having enough milk for your coffee, can be described as 'management failures' – and if you cannot pin a management failure on anyone else, you might have to accept it as your own. If your train is late, it is a failure in operational management by the rail company, but if you are late for your train, your own failure in time management is to blame.

The fact is that we are all managers – the managers of our own lives, whether or not we like to think of it that way – but that does not mean we can all be taught to be successful managers. Just as some leaders are born rather than trained, there are people on whom management courses or, indeed, any formal 'education', are wasted. These often turn out to be the best managers because their heads aren't cluttered with arcane theory and impenetrable jargon.

Managing even a big organisation is only an application of the basic principles you have learnt in managing your own day-to-day existence. Most management really is just common sense. However, over the years the 'common' has grown into 'specific', where different areas of the organisation require different management skills. You do not have to worry about obtaining an in-depth understanding of these different disciplines; you just need to know about the concepts that are common to them all – so it really is *common* sense.

An overview of each of the different areas of management will enable you to appear extremely knowledgeable about your fellow managers' areas of expertise (assuming, of course, that they really are genuine specialist managers, dedicated to their own areas of expertise, and not, like you, expert only in the art of bluffing).

To outsmart your peers, subordinates and superiors, you can use this book to learn useful management tools and mantras which you should utilise by dropping them into conversation whenever possible. Of course, you are not expected to make use of them yourself, but armed with the management skills of delegation and staff empowerment, you will be amazed at how you will be able to guide your staff to use the tools to get results that you can then use to impress others.

How can a bluffer pass as a real manager? Remarkably easily. Very few managers think seriously about their actions, objectives and motives. Anyone devoting even a fragment of the working day to cerebral activity about how to be a better manager stands out as a dangerous revolutionary. People above them on the corporate ladder see this sort of reckless individualism at best as a catalyst for change (which nobody likes) and at worst as a threat to their own positions.

The perfect manager seeks to rise above the herd while, at the same time, appearing to desire nothing more than to remain part of it. You need to be seen as a 'team player' if you are to effectively lead the team, but you must also separate yourself from mere followers in thought, word and deed – without anyone noticing what you are doing. As comedian George Burns said: 'Sincerity is everything. If you can fake that, you've got it made.'

This book sets out to guide you through the main danger zones where you are most likely to encounter tricky management challenges. It will equip you with the vocabulary and evasive techniques required to distinguish yourself as a manager of rare ability and experience and to minimise your risk of being found out as a bluffer. In other words, it will enable you to impress legions of marvelling listeners with your knowledge and advice – without anyone discovering that you couldn't actually manage a village paper round.

A WORKING TITLE

Your first decision in management is the most important: where do you want to bluff? The born bluffer will of course aim straight for the top. There is, after all, always room there. However, there is also always vicious in-fighting there too, between some of the most cunning and competitive people in the world. So you might prefer to look for a niche a little lower down, where you can be monarch of your own private empire.

The importance of your choice of title cannot be overstressed. Note that it is your choice. Your employers may be under the quaint impression that they choose what to call you, but this is true only if you let them. What you call yourself defines how others see you and how you see yourself. Title is in fact a self-fulfilling prophecy: if you sound important, you will be important.

Your first step is to ignore the official title when you introduce yourself. Describe yourself as you would ideally like to be seen and you will soon be seen as just that. If, therefore, your official title is 'office manager', start thinking of yourself as 'systems director'.

Needless to say, this all becomes superfluous if you really do happen to have an impressive title. Then your tactic should be one of deliberate understatement. 'Oh, I help with the books at Universal Widgets' is fine when it can be followed by the immediate presentation of the business card which reveals you as group finance director.

It therefore follows that you must proceed with great care in choosing the title to which you aspire. Or decide to avoid.

The following list might help; it is not exhaustive.

CHAIRMAN

Most organisations are headed by a person with some variant on the splendidly democratic title of chairman*. This implies an egalitarian body of whom the chairman is one among equals and just happens to be the one who chairs meetings. This is, of course, a caricature of the more common reality in which a chairman runs things about as democratically as Vlad the Impaler. Yet, for legal reasons there is usually a body, such as a board of directors, which the chairman chairs and with whom he nominally shares power. Since most members of these bodies are, in practice, appointed to their lucrative sinecures with the chairman's approval, the result is rarely Classical Athens in terms of open debate.

* In the private sector, the title is 'chairman', even when the chairman is a woman. In the public sector, which is run by left-leaning employees even when the right is in power, expressions like 'chairperson', 'chair' or 'chairwoman' are used, according to fashion.

Confusingly, in US companies there is often a president below the chairman – despite there being no chairman above the president of the United States. Even more confusingly, British organisations often have an honorary president nominally above the chairman but with no real power in the hierarchy, in much the same manner as the Queen is supposed to outrank a prime minister but still does basically as she is told.

The title vice president is handed out generally to make people feel better about themselves without meaning very much. Again, there is an obvious parallel here with the federal government of the USA, except that most organisations can have as many vice presidents as they want. Whether even one is necessary is another matter.

The title chairman is obviously very desirable to the bluffer. Alas, there is only one proper chairman per organisation. However, the chairman of a subsidiary board, committee or sub-committee might emphasise the word 'chairman' and neglect to mention the bit that comes afterwards.

CHIEF EXECUTIVE

Whatever the chairman's delusions of grandeur, the chief executive is the person who actually runs things. The chairman may not be a full-time employee of the organisation; indeed he may be no more than a front for the chief executive. Alternatively, the real megalomaniac will combine the offices of chairman and chief executive.

Chief executives used to have humbler titles, usually managing director in the UK or general manager in the

USA. Most these days cannot resist the combination of the powerful 'chief' with the dynamic 'executive' in the same title. More impressive still is the variant used in the USA, chief executive officer – often abbreviated to the even more dramatic acronym, CEO.

As a general rule, you really have arrived when you no longer even have a title and are described instead by a set of letters. Real power increases in direct proportion to the decrease in the number of letters by which you are referred. Deputy and assistant directors have longer titles, and therefore more letters, than their superiors, so that an assistant director of finance and administration might be ADFA, and the director DFA. It seems an unwritten rule that no one has fewer than three letters in a private organisation, presumably in order to avoid offending the CEO. Two letters, like PM or HM, implies national prominence. Napoleon just used N. M, of course, gives out licences to kill. Many CEOs would secretly love to do the same.

C LEVEL

The goal of ambitious people in a hierarchy used to be 'board level' or 'director level' (see below). Now, more and more, it is 'C level'. Not to be outdone by CEOs, finance directors became chief financial officers or CFOs, operating directors became chief operations officers or COOs, and so on. Now it seems there is no limit to the possible C levels in an organisation. We now have titles like chief technical officer, chief legal officer, chief creative officer, chief risk officer, chief learning officer, chief brand officer, chief knowledge officer and even – surely a contradiction in terms in any hierarchy – chief visionary officer. Followers of *Star Trek* will feel vindicated by the fact that the posts of chief science officer and chief communications officer really do exist in many organisations.

As a general rule, you really have arrived when you no longer even have a title and are described instead by a set of letters.

The advantage of C level from the bluffer's perspective is that it implies the highest possible rank in the organisation but is not tied to any particular level in the hierarchy. You do not have to be at board level or even manager level to have a C-level title; if you narrow your specialisation enough so that you are indeed the senior person performing that particular function in the whole organisation, then you can claim to be chief of that function in the organisation. So the tea boy in the cashier's office becomes the organisation's chief financial services beverage supply officer and the janitor in reception the chief front office cleansing officer.

This 'title inflation' is a long-established and apparently universal phenomena. Equivalents can be found in ancient Rome, where it seems everyone got to be consul by the end. Perhaps that is why the empire declined and fell.

As each title becomes desirable, more and more people aspire to it. Before long, they either assume it themselves or they are granted it by their indulgent superiors – usually in lieu of a pay rise. Then the title becomes so commonplace that everyone desires something better. Thus, clerks became assistants, then assistants became officers, then officers became managers, then managers became directors, and now directors are becoming chiefs.

So it will continue until all of us have the job title supreme grand emperor – and then a higher title will have to be invented.

DIRECTORS

Directors are, legally, the members of the governing board of a company. They tend to guard their prerogatives jealously. For the same reason, the title is desirable to bluffers. Of course, it is easy enough to get – anyone can set up their own company – but since everyone knows this it will hardly be much of an achievement. Getting the title 'director' from a large organisation, implying that you are on the main or group board, without actually being on it, should therefore be the goal of the management bluffer.

The cheap compromise is to start calling yourself associate director or deputy director, then accidentally dropping the associate or deputy bit, but this is surely beneath the true bluffer. Instead, describe yourself as director not of the company but of a particular facility or department. Few would really argue that 'laboratory director' is not an appropriate title for 'laboratory manager' because laboratories do not tend to have directors running them. If challenged, you can reply, 'Director describes my function, not my rank', which is technically correct.

Best of all, get on to one of the company's subsidiary boards. Most companies have lots of subsidiary companies, some of them nominally on the books just to prevent someone else using a name that might be confused with the company or its products. Offer to undertake the laborious task of serving on one of their nominal boards and attending a five-minute annual meeting every year. You can then say, truthfully, 'I'm a director with Mega-Global Industries', without being a director *of* Mega-Global Industries.

FINANCE DIRECTOR

All companies have someone who does the books. They rarely call themselves bookkeepers; 'chief cashier' has a better air of Dickensian authority. Alternatively, the widely preferred 'finance director' sounds modern and dynamic. 'FD' sounds even more so.

The joy of being finance director (or manager) is that it implies professional status even if you are just, well, a bookkeeper. There is nothing stopping you being 'chief accountant' even if you are not, in any technical or legal sense, an accountant.

You can even be 'director of finance and administration', implying both legal and financial expertise. The two have often been combined. Finance director was often traditionally combined with the statutory post of company secretary. The latter title tends to be de-emphasised these days, as the once honourable title of secretary – 'keeper of secrets' – has fallen into disfavour even among secretaries who prefer being personal assistants (PAs).

Of course, the bluffer will naturally be drawn to the US title, chief financial officer, with its acronym, CFO.

OPERATIONS DIRECTOR

Production managers or directors used to enjoy enormous status, so it says something about the strange elitism of today that people in their positions prefer the quasi-military titles of operations manager or director. It is at least in part due to the fact that so many, perhaps most, companies these days do not have a product in the tangible sense. Operations certainly describes the process of the delivery of a service better than production.

Operations covers all aspects of providing whatever it is the organisation is meant to provide in return for its money. It is about what the organisation was supposedly set up to do, as opposed to administration and marketing which are, in theory at least, only support functions, even if this is usually forgotten in practice. In the USA, the chief operating officer (COO) will form a triumvirate with the CEO and CFO at the head of the organisation.

Yet the bluffer is generally advised to steer clear of operations. The obligation to provide everything the organisation is supposed to provide means that you will be expected to:

a) actually know things
b) actually do things.

This is not what bluffers are meant to do.

MARKETING DIRECTOR

This is more like the bluffer's home turf because marketing is basically all bluffing. For a start, marketing itself comes down to the plain old business of selling. The marketing director, of course, can never admit that. You have to be ready with all the jargon about product placement, USPs, segmentation, customer profiles, POS, distribution strategy and the like. In other words, you have to bluff.

Of course, there is no avoiding that you still have to learn the jargon, but that takes about an afternoon, whereas an operations director might have to study engineering, management science, operational research and all sorts of specialist stuff for years. Indeed, there are shortcuts to save even those few hours: make up your own jargon. The odds are that most people you encounter in marketing are in no position to challenge your assumed 'expertise'.

The other great thing about marketing is that, since it is full of bluffers, titles proliferate like nowhere else. It is easier to be a manager or director in marketing than anywhere else. Regional sales managers often have no one to manage.

HUMAN RESOURCES DIRECTOR

This is another role that has grown enormously in self-importance in recent times. This is basically old-fashioned 'personnel management' given a pompous new name.

The growth of HR, as it calls itself (note two letters), has been aided by the increase in legal obligations on employers, combined with a lot of trendy management theory about how it might be more efficient not to treat all employees like cattle.

From the bluffer's point of view, learning all the legal stuff could be hard work, but the management theory stuff is fairly elementary, and as easy to pick up, and make up, as the marketing jargon.

Be warned, however, that HR is rarely the best route to status and respect within an organisation. HR managers are often seen as the enemy within, going on about legal obligations and good practice. Line managers – people who head actual groups of people in operational departments – also do not consider them to be proper managers since they, the line managers, are the ones doing the managing.

The only time a line manager really finds an HR director useful is when he needs an axe-man to lay people off. Then the HR director is suddenly popular with the line manager – and no one else – as years of progressive HR practice suddenly count for nothing.

Bluffers should note that there is a worrying trend in the USA to conflate HR with something known as 'talent management' (TM), defined by John Hopkins University in Baltimore as 'a set of integrated organizational HR processes designed to attract, develop, motivate, and retain productive, engaged employees'. This is also known in English as 'hiring and firing'.

TOTAL QUALITY MANAGER

The old idea of 'quality assurance' became briefly very popular not so long ago when it reinvented itself as 'total quality management'. This was based on the clever notion – Japanese, of course – that one should look not only at the quality of the product but at the process that produced it.

The idea was generally adopted but the novelty soon wore off. Line managers, again conscious that they are still the ones doing the actual managing, tend to view TQM specialists, like HR specialists, as jumped-up inspectors and not 'real' managers.

TQM attracted many ambitious bluffers but is now out of fashion. The artistic bluffer should instead be looking for the next fashionable management theory.

BRAND MANAGER

Brand management brings specialists from different parts of an organisation together to market and produce a specific brand. Since, as a bluffer, you are effectively marketing yourself as a brand, this may come naturally to you. However, if it does not, it is not a safe place to be; it is very difficult to hide from the results.

PROJECT MANAGER

Like brand management, project management brings together specialists from different parts of an organisation for a common purpose but with the crucial difference that it is temporary.

Projects usually involve initiating change in some way – restructuring, building a new plant or developing a new product. This can be quite good fun. The concept of any sort of change, however, is not always universally popular, and must be handled carefully.

Many bluffers have made careers out of project management, hopping from one interesting project to the next. The trick is to keep moving, so any negative consequences from your last project never catch up with you.

CUSTOMER SERVICE MANAGER

The expression 'customer service' is a bluff in its own right. What we are talking about here is the complaints department – often combined, significantly, with the bad debts department. Providing a service to the customer usually has little to do with it.

The work itself involves a great deal of bluff – convincing unhappy customers that everything will be all right, that the organisation is working efficiently to solve all problems, and that it in fact gives a damn.

The title 'manager' is given out here in much the same way that inexperienced young pilots got commissioned just before they got shot down, and anyone who goes into customer service with the idea of serving people is more likely to have been bluffed than be a bluffer.

SERVICES (IT) MANAGER

In recent years this role has fallen under the aegis of the DDS (*see* below). The old office manager – often a person of not inconsiderable power and prestige – is now usually the services manager, who tends to have a lower status. The role is often combined with that of the information technology (IT) manager, possibly under the title systems manager.

IT management is the fast track. Most managers are frightened by IT; they know next to nothing about it and are fearfully impressed by anyone who can switch a computer on correctly. So the geeky teenager who has, undoubtedly, spent too much time surfing the net may find captains of industry looking up to him in awe. The title 'IT manager' may be bestowed on some callow youth with no actual people to manage, it being generally accepted that managing those mystifying machines is more than enough to justify the title.

It is therefore an area that should interest the bluffer who knows something about Boolean logic functions, mail transfer protocols, and JavaScript. You do not have to know much; a grasp of the more familiar jargon and the confidence to bluff the rest, combined with a grasp of the very few basic functions for which most computers are used, should win you the respect of the whole organisation. But beware the DDS whose brief is far-reaching and all-embracing.

RISK MANAGER

Risk management, of course, is not management at all. It is risk assessment, a minor function easily carried out by a reasonably numerate subordinate. Yet it is a good example of how the title 'manager' has expanded. A 'real' manager is a line manager, one who manages a group of people – usually a group large enough to have subordinates acting as supervisors over other subordinates. As such, it is a position and title worthy of status and prestige.

Others desire that status and prestige. Many organisations have consequently found it useful to award the title 'manager' to key employees who are not actually managing anything or anyone.

It is therefore not surprising that people in less illustrious roles, like risk assessors, personnel officers, complaints managers, quality inspectors and computer geeks, should seek to upgrade whatever they do to 'management' and therefore themselves, by logical extension, to 'managers'. The bluffer must deplore this – and seek to do the same.

Eventually you will become what you pretend to be.

DIRECTOR OF CORPORATE AFFAIRS

Nobody knows exactly what this person does, least of all the director of corporate affairs. Generally speaking their job description is much the same as that of the communications director, and nobody knows what they do either.

On paper the DCA is responsible for creating and communicating a favourable public image for his employer or client, but given the opportunity he or she will drone on about the job function not only safeguarding the corporate reputation, but also about being strategists and architects of a 'proactive' corporate narrative and its dissemination across all platforms and audiences. Exactly. The younger DCA will probably have a degree in media studies and will therefore profess to know the media world inside out – notwithstanding that they will have virtually no useful and biddable contacts in journalism, and no leverage over the less scrupulous members of the press. Generally speaking their job is relatively untaxing until the CEO suddenly decides that the company needs a flattering personal profile of him/her in the *Financial Times*. At this point the DCA passes the task to the agency handling the company's public relations and blames them when they come up with a single column inch in the *Daily Mail*'s City pages which gleefully reports that the CEO is on the lookout for a new job (shortly to be followed by the DCA).

DIRECTOR OF DIGITAL STRATEGY

Another improbable pretender clambering up the corporate ladder, the DDS is ideally placed to have the ear of the chairman, the CEO, the FD, COO and just about any other well-nourished acronym too scared to admit that they're completely out of sync with the digital world. (Or rather, 'space'.) He (and it is almost always a he) has convinced the board that he can do little wrong, because nobody else in the company understands anything about IT apart from the IT manager who 'reports into' the DDS and is routinely ignored by him until something goes wrong and someone has to be blamed. The DDS actually knows very little about anything (and certainly doesn't dirty his hands with mundane IT problems) but he shrouds his ignorance in mystifying jargon and endless meetings about 'digital horizon objectives'.

It matters not to senior management that he speaks in an alien tongue and is probably a Russian avatar whose cerebral cortex has a habit of regularly misfiring. If you ever see a DDS overheating in a meeting, which he calls a 'digital content huddle' while saying 'we need to benchmark our agile organic search with a one-size-fits-all yet disruptive customer relationship lifecycle', or just repeating 'core competencies' over and over again with the faint smell of something burning, you've probably got a faulty one and should send it back to the manufacturers. But in today's all-consuming gold-rush for the mythical grail of digital revenues from social media and the web, wiring issues aside the DDS is practically untouchable because he has convinced his superiors that without his knowledge and expertise the organisation will grind to a halt. Or even worse: the newly 'digital-first' company will fail to prioritise an exponential week-on-week revenue growth across fully responsive online traffic verticals and robust metrics. (See what we mean?) The DDS is in fact an example of a worrying development in the world of management, because he/she is a consummate bluffer. Unfortunately he is a bluffer-gone-bad. Beware.

THE DEMANDS OF LEADERSHIP

Much of what is today called 'management' used to be called 'administration'. That is why the most prestigious management degree is still called the MBA, the Masters of Business Administration. In time, however, 'administration' came to be associated with red tape and bureaucracy, while management sounded relatively modern and dynamic and sexy.

In much the same way, and for much the same reasons, the word 'management' is, in its turn, being supplanted by the word 'leadership'. After all, 'manager' evokes images of a man in a suit, 'administrator' of a man in a pullover or even a cardigan, and 'leader' of a man in battle armour, leading his mighty host against the enemy. This association is rather flattering to the contemporary middle manager. His fantasising is nurtured by a vast and increasing leadership literature that encourages him to consider himself as the successor of Napoleon, Alexander the Great, Zun Tzu or Genghis Khan.

For all that, just as there are differences between administration and management, there are differences between management and leadership. The big difference is the role of other people. Leadership is all about the interaction between the leader and a group of other people known as followers. Without the followers, there is no leader and thus no leadership. The problem is that, while there is no shortage of people willing to put themselves forward as leaders, few want to think of themselves as followers. As often as not, the trick is to get people to follow without them realising that they *are* following.

Leadership is part – often a very big part – of the work of most managers, but there is more to management than that. Management is the whole process of running something. If there are others involved then leadership is a necessary aspect of the task, but it is not the only aspect. There are some things that cannot be delegated to others – and top of that list is responsibility. It should also be noted that even the smallest enterprises, run by and employing only a single individual, still need to be managed and, indeed, administered.

So the bluffer should make the most of the fashionable cult of 'leadership', but not take it too seriously.

THE CHALLENGE OF LEADERSHIP

The very idea of leading others remains daunting to many, including those who are good self-managers in the sense that they are very well organised when it comes to their own work.

This is where bluffing comes into its own. More than any other sphere of human activity, leadership relies on a bluff. Sometimes the greatest leaders have admitted as much. Historical biographies are full of famous orators being physically sick with nerves before making their speeches and mighty warlords smitten with uncertainty the night before their battles. Napoleon (note that you should always quote Napoleon in any discussion of leadership) said that he had often seen courage on the battlefield but real courage was 'two o'clock in the morning' courage and was very rare indeed.

Note that Napoleon did not actually say that he had such courage himself. The point is that it is not really necessary to have it at all; you only have to persuade others that you do. The career of Napoleon shows that he was himself a highly successful and well-practised bluffer. So to be a great leader you do not have to be Napoleon. You do not even have to pretend to be Napoleon. You only have to persuade others that you are the man Napoleon pretended to be.

That may be easier than you might imagine....

THE GREAT SECRET OF LEADERSHIP

There is a secret to all forms of leadership that can be summed up in a single sentence: 'The true way to be popular with the troops is not to be free and familiar with them, but to make them believe you know more than they do.'

This remark is attributed to the American General William T. Sherman. Whether he actually said it or not is beside the point. Sherman was the man who marched an army through the heart of the Confederacy and who later declined the presidency of the United States. They named a tank after him. He is therefore, like Napoleon, the sort of person a bluffer should mention when discussing leadership.

Indeed, we might as well go all the way and give the remark an academic-sounding name like 'Sherman's Dictum'. Management experts are always giving impressive titles to statements of the obvious; the more self-confident put their own names on them and turn them into bestselling books. This is all bluffing on a grand scale.

The fact remains that, whoever said it, that one little sentence really does sum up everything you need to know about leadership. It contains two separate but related ideas, and it might be worth taking a bit of time to think about what they mean in practice.

'It cannot be stressed enough that the appearance of knowledge is more important than the knowledge itself.'

The first part of Sherman's Dictum is a warning against being too free and familiar with subordinates. This may seem contrary to modern ideas of democratic management, in which everyone calls each other by their first names and all socialise together. Yet there is a lot of truth in the old saying that 'familiarity breeds contempt'. The corollary of this is that respect increases with distance. This does not mean one has to be a snob or a bully when dealing with subordinates, but there is such a thing as getting too close. It is certainly very difficult if you find that you have to discipline someone who is a regular drinking buddy with whom you have shared your deepest secrets. So the ideal is to aim at being 'friendly but not familiar'.

If you can carry this off, it is of great assistance when it comes to implementing the second half of Sherman's Dictum, which is persuading your subordinates that you know something they do not.

It is truly said that 'knowledge is power'. Sherman understood that soldiers, in the confusion of combat, obey their officers because they assume that their officers know more about the objective and how to achieve it with minimal loss. Anyone in a dangerous situation will follow the person who seems to best know how to get them out of that situation safely. People in a democracy vote for the politician or the party projecting the best impression of knowing how to run things. Investors will back the entrepreneur who appears to know how to make money. In every case, authority relies not on rank or title or legal status but on knowledge, or at least the appearance of knowledge.

For it cannot be stressed enough that, at least in this context, the appearance of knowledge is more important than the knowledge itself. Knowledgeable people are often very bad at communicating how knowledgeable they are. They may be the sort of people who spend so much time reading books that they do not develop social skills. Or their superior knowledge may only lead them to the realisation that they know very little relative to what they do not know – a profound philosophical truth, but not one that builds the appearance of self-confidence demanded in a leader.

So there are two ways to appear more knowledgeable than your subordinates. The first is to acquire superior knowledge and combine it with the appearance of self-confidence. The second is to bluff.

LEADERSHIP AND KNOWLEDGE

While it certainly helps to be all-knowing, it is by no means essential.

It all comes down to timing. Rather than attempt to impress with a constant flow of knowledge, the bluffer should develop the technique of surprising subordinates with well-chosen nuggets of relevant information when they least expect it.

As a manager, you can bluff your subordinates into assuming that you are more knowledgeable than you actually are by choosing the right moments to raise intelligent points and ask them intelligent questions. That will keep them on their toes at all times, because they will not know when you will put them to the test.

The right moments are the rare moments when you happen to know what you are talking about. Those moments may be few and far between, but they will be enough. They will be remembered. There is nothing more shocking to a subordinate than to be surprised by an incisive point or question coming from a manager who was previously written off as an idiot. In a single moment, all the subordinate's previous assumptions are undermined, and they become very wary about making such assumptions in future. You need only catch a subordinate unawares once or twice to ensure that they will always treat you with respect in the future.

This technique is effective only if you preserve the strictest self-discipline by never attempting to use it unless you are absolutely certain about what you're saying. If there is the slightest doubt, keep your mouth shut. What impresses is not the number of intelligent points you raise but the fact that, however many points you raise, they are always sound. What you want is not a reputation for breadth of knowledge but for infallibility. To do that you cannot afford to be caught saying something remotely fatuous even once. Resist the temptation to impress by piling on the points based on information you think is probably true. That 'probably' is not good enough – you must be certain or you must be silent.

It is important, however, not to go to the other extreme of never saying anything at all. As Sir Winston Churchill once said, 'Too often the strong, silent man is silent because he does not know what to say, and is reputed strong only because he remains silent.'

So silence can be useful, but only in the short term. Sooner or later, the silent manager will be put on the spot – and, if there is nothing behind the silence, exposed.

To avoid this, you must use the manager's privilege of choosing the moment. Take the initiative by ambushing each of your subordinates at least once early in your relationship. Do your research and prepare a single good question in advance that tests their specialist expertise and suggests that you know their subject as well as they do.

If your question flummoxes your subordinate, do not be nasty or triumphalist: just give an indulgent, almost parental, smile and move on....

If, on the other hand, the question provokes a good answer, or one that you do not understand but sounds clever, do not enter a debate; just nod sagely and give the same enigmatic smile. If you have a beard, stroke it ruminatively.

LEADERSHIP AND RESEARCH

Although the whole point of bluffing is to avoid having to actually know everything, a successful bluff does demand some research. You do not need to know everything but you need to know just enough.

The bluffer should make it a rule never to go into a meeting without at least one good point and at least one good question properly prepared in advance. It is not necessary to use them – certainly not every time – but better to have and not need them than to need them and not have them.

Search engines and online encyclopedias are very useful in this respect – although it should never be forgotten that everyone else knows this. It is more than possible that a specialist in a specific area will be able to recognise information that comes from the Wikipedia entry on the subject or from the top Google result. Nor should it be forgotten that the accuracy of Wikipedia and other internet sources is, to put it politely, variable. It is not unknown for people who know or suspect that their boss relies on Wikipedia to alter an entry; a boss who starts spouting the same bogus nonsense that the smirking subordinate put online will lose all credibility and is unlikely to regain it.

So, where possible, cross-check your sources and, wherever you have a choice of reliable sources, use the more obscure. If all this sounds like hard work, it need only take a few minutes before each meeting and is well worth the effort.

Where the meeting is to discuss a specific document, the bluffer need not read it all, especially if it is long and boring and technical. Your role as manager is only to make sure the subordinate has read it. So select a couple of pages in the middle at random, and prepare a couple of detailed points or questions on whatever you happen to find there. They may be totally unimportant but the subordinate will assume they are important because you raised them.

LEADERSHIP AND CONTROL

A leader has only two real obligations: to set subordinates clear and specific tasks, and to make sure they perform them.

The defining of tasks is the more difficult because it does require a degree of aptitude that the bluffer might or might not possess, but it need not demand originality. If the leader is part of a management hierarchy with superior managers above, the obvious strategy is to simply pass on whatever comes from above to the subordinates below. This will have the double benefit of pleasing the superiors and covering the bluffer.

If, on the other hand, the leader is the head of the organisation, it is hard to avoid having to use initiative – hard, but not impossible. The solution is to ask the subordinates themselves what they think they should be doing. This can be very effective because, as a general rule, the people closest to a task know most about it.

The problem is managing to do this without appearing weak in front of the subordinates. One method might be to pass it off as consultation, as part of a 'democratic' style of management. Better still is to imply that it is some sort of test of their mettle. In the British television comedy *Dad's Army*, the nominal leader, Captain Mainwaring, was not the most intellectual of men but he was an instinctive bluffer who would exploit this technique whenever one of his subordinates had a good idea, usually with the words, 'I was wondering who'd be the first to spot that.'

Of course, the joke was that poor Mainwaring could never quite carry it off – it was always obvious that the idea was new to him – but the technique can be very effective in the hands of the more subtle bluffer. A knowing smile and a nod of approval might be enough, especially if the subordinates have already been softened up by the well-timed demonstrations of knowledge mentioned above.

Having assigned tasks to your subordinates, it is important to give the appearance of keeping on top of them to make sure those tasks are performed. Once again, the important word here is 'appearance'. You need only plan a couple of well-prepared and well-planned interventions to keep a subordinate on the alert. Just as someone seems to be getting complacent about their work, surprise them with a question about it to which only you know the answer. In legal circles, one of the first rules of the art of cross-examination is: never ask a question to which you do not know the answer. This axiom is just as relevant in a management context.

LEADERSHIP AND ETHICS

A good manager always has to control subordinates, sometimes has to exploit them, but never has to be cruel to them. The nasty, aggressive style of management one frequently encounters is wholly counterproductive – and doubly counterproductive to the bluffer. If you make your subordinates your adversaries, they will always be trying to catch you out, and to a bluffer that means they will always be trying to catch you in a bluff. One day they will succeed, if they are motivated to try hard enough.

The best way to avoid this is to give them no reason to try. Sherman said a leader should not be free and familiar with subordinates, but that does not mean that he should go out of his way to be hated. It costs nothing to be affable. Once you have established the necessary dominance over a subordinate, there is no reason to intimidate. Shouting, bad language and temper tantrums are all symptoms of bad leadership.

Loss of personal control leads to loss of organisational control. Sarcasm serves no purpose. Politeness is always appreciated, especially when it is not strictly necessary. Do not flatter subordinates unduly, but give praise where it is due. Be firm but know that there are times to loosen the reins a little. Little gestures of unforced kindness and generosity can go a long way – so long as they are not so frequent that they become taken for granted and their absence resented. Be sparing with the honey, but a little sweetness can balance the sour.

Even if the worst comes to the worst, an amiable bluffer can always laugh off being caught in a bluff – if only once or twice; beyond that there is real risk to credibility. By contrast, a bully caught bluffing will be given no slack at all. News of the bully's humiliation will be spread with glee throughout the organisation and repeated constantly so that it is not forgotten. No amount of bluster can recover authority lost this way.

All of which brings the bluffer to the controversial subject of...

A QUESTION OF STYLE

There is endless literature of the subject of management style. Most of it is bunkum. All the various theories and labels describe the same basic styles and they don't really help you change yours. Make sure you know the difference between a Theory X and a Theory Y type and you'll know enough. There are many types of manager – directive, authoritarian, supportive, participative, consultative – but it is likely that you will fall into one of two mindsets: autocratic or democratic.

THE AUTOCRATIC MANAGER

This is the traditional hard-nosed boss. He tends to subscribe to 'Theory X', the notion that all workers are inherently lazy and will not work unless managed with a firm hand.

A good case study of this type of management in action can be observed in the galley scene of the film *Ben Hur*. Typically this manager is driven by profit and likes to keep on top of every situation. As has already been pointed out, this is a dangerous option for the bluffer because it increases both the chances of being exposed and the negative consequences when it happens.

THE DEMOCRATIC MANAGER

The democratic manager is one who is more genial than hard-nosed, is supportive and considerate of staff and participates in many work activities with the team. This manager usually has a touching faith in 'Theory Y', which suggests that workers are in fact human beings and can be encouraged to motivate themselves to work.

Most of the vast academic literature, and not a few bestsellers, support Theory Y over Theory X – and, for the most part, rightly so. In practice, however, the issues are not quite so clear-cut.

For a start, the response of many real-life managers to the academics and bestsellers is 'Well, they would say that, wouldn't they?' After all, no one is going to sell many books with a title *Treat Your Employees Like The Scum They Are*. Nor are academics likely to research best practice in sweat shops.

There is also the undeniable fact that some jobs are simply not fun and little can be done to alter that fact. They still have to be done, and the only reason anyone is prepared to do them is because they need the money. In those circumstances, a manager who tries too hard to jolly his people along will strike a jarringly false note.

Finally, there is such a thing as trying too hard to be liked. The irony here is that those who are too needy end up being despised. This is certainly true in management.

All other things being equal, subordinates actually tend to prefer a strong leader to a weak one. Strength is by no means incompatible with a democratic management style, but there is a danger that being too open and accommodating may be perceived as weakness (*see* Sherman's Dictum, above).

All that having been said, as a general rule, consultation and delegation are very useful management tools, and the basis of a sensible management strategy more often than not – especially for the bluffer. If you really have no idea what you are doing, as advised earlier, you can always let your subordinates decide for you and still make it look like good management practice.

MANAGEMENT V BULLYING

Whatever style of management you choose, even if you go for a more autocratic style – perhaps especially if you go for a more autocratic style – you must be on guard against any form of bullying.

Bullying is a very visible sign of inadequacy; apart from anything else, it destroys in an instant the impression of self-confidence and authority the bluffer seeks to project. Bullies have usually been bullied themselves, and they try to hide their weakness and work out their frustrations by bullying others in turn. An organisation tends to develop a culture according to the standards set at the top, so if there is bullying at the top, there will be bullying all the way down. Those at the bottom will have no one to bully, so, in a commercial organisation, they will take it out on their customers; in a government organisation, they will take it out on the public. Anyone who has had extensive dealings with many national tax authorities will confirm the truth of this.

In addition to the moral consequences, bullying can also now have significant legal (and financial) consequences – for the organisation, for those involved and, most importantly here, for any manager who is perceived as not doing enough to prevent it. Forget any mental images of big children beating up little children for their lunch money; the definition of bullying – and its siblings, harassment and discrimination – is getting wider and wider. In some jurisdictions these days, it seems you only have to look at someone in a way they do not like for them to sue you. It does not matter if such a case has little merit; the costs and inconvenience of litigation mean that many organisations find it easier to settle. When they do, they tend to take it out, in turn, on the manager who allowed the mess to develop. When that happens, it is no use for the manager to argue that the law is now too broad, and anyway it was the organisation's decision to settle – which may very well be true but hardly alters the fact that someone has to take the blame.

The sort of people who become bluffers are not, generally speaking, the sort of people who become bullies. Bluffers are far too easygoing and averse to confrontation. The real challenge for the bluffer in management is to prevent subordinates bullying each other. This is very hard because they are hardly likely to do it in front of their manager. Where they do, or where bullying is reported, swift, decisive, even ruthless suppression of the bully is the safest course – but that still leaves the real problem of hidden bullying.

Here, a slight variant on the techniques outlined in the 'Management and Leadership' chapters might come in useful. Identify those who you think, whether fairly or unfairly, could possibly develop into bullies, whether on the basis of their position or some personal characteristics you have noted. Then, invite them in, one by one, for 'a little confidential chat' – without letting anyone else know. They will probably be a little nervous, not knowing what the meeting is about. Without warning, you then launch into a calm and reasoned monologue on the evils of bullying in the workplace but – and this is the important point – only in the most general terms and in the most friendly tone of voice.

It seems you only have to look at someone in a way they do not like for them to sue you.

Most will take it as a standard warning that does not apply to them. However, those guilty of bullying may be alarmed. Once again, they will wonder if you know more than you are saying. They will become paranoid about you watching them. They will, if they have any brains at all, treat it as a subtle hint to desist and – not knowing the limits of your knowledge – usually take the hint.

The key to this is that you have already used the techniques described before to build up your reputation among your subordinates as someone who knows a great deal more than you let on. For the same reason, your 'little chat' may have the opposite effect on others and prompt them to report that they are being bullied. Either way, this is a form of the old military tactic known as 'reconnaissance by fire' – i.e., if you do not know if an enemy is hiding in a bush, fire at the bush, and if the bush fires back, then you know the enemy is there.

MANAGING COLLEAGUES

Fortunately, few of your colleagues have been trained to manage. The few who know about it in theory revert to type in a crisis and frequently forget all they have learnt, or think it doesn't apply to them. It follows that basic competence as a bluffer will put you ahead of most managers, trained and untrained. This implies that you may be role-playing much of the time. For most imperfect mortals that is the essence of management.

MANAGING SUPERIORS

In an organisational hierarchy there is only one serious option regarding relations with superiors, assuming you want to remain in that hierarchy and progress in it: total subservience.

That said, obvious crawling is counterproductive – because it is obvious. Your strategy is therefore to make a big show of how independent-minded you are, but somehow the conclusion to which your independent mind always comes just happens to be the same conclusion reached by your boss.

The ideal is to cultivate a reputation for plain-speaking while never actually saying anything controversial: 'I will quite understand if you fire me for saying this, Boss, but I have to tell you that you're absolutely right.'

MANAGING OFFICE POLITICS

The situation is obviously far more difficult if you have several superiors or potential superiors. The sensible thing is to be polite and deferential to them all. If forced to take sides, always go with the strongest, but try to avoid any assignment that involves having to be really hard on a weaker player. You never know who is going to be the strongest tomorrow.

Above all, be nice to everyone on your way up because you never know who you are going to need on your way back down.

The need to have an opinion will almost invariably involve a flow of data from your inquisitor, who might be subordinate, supplier, boss or customer.

THE MANAGEMENT SKILL SET

There will be times when even a bluffer is faced with the need to take a position about something, anything, in management. There is a rule for such times – not a golden one but plated thick enough to pass – which is all that counts for the bluffer: when someone asks for your opinion, try to get theirs first. The need to have an opinion will almost invariably involve a flow of data from your inquisitor, who might be subordinate, supplier, boss or customer. The correct posture is the professional one of wanting to know enough about the circumstances before you volunteer an opinion.

Ask some 'Who, What, When, Where, Why' questions (WWWWW) while you are giving it 'headspace' (*see* 'Jargon and Glossary'). Some of these are bound to be answered sloppily, so ask for a 'more objective input'. Even if this is forthcoming, there may be the chance to point out politely that what you seek are facts rather than opinions. This will give you more time to strive to form an opinion of your own. When you get facts, it may be permissible to ask for evidence, just in case these facts are still actually opinions.

By this time several things may have happened. Your colleagues may have realised in the process of explaining the situation what the solution is. Or they may have shown that there isn't a problem. Or, by the grace of God, you may have realised what is wrong yourself. Don't think this is just bluff. The process is quite like real management and you will get credit for doing it this way.

There are endless lists of 'key skills' supposedly required by managers. If you have read this far, you will have worked out that the only skill that really matters is the ability to choose your moment carefully and keep your mouth shut the rest of the time. Get that right and you will develop the reputation of being a 'sound fellow' and a 'safe pair of hands', which is a better way to the top of most organisations than brilliance or excellence or any of those other virtues that bosses praise loudly but view with extreme suspicion.

So long as that is firmly understood, it probably does no actual harm to be at least aware of other management skills. Look out for them in others, and make use of them if a situation arises in which they might be helpful to you; just do not imagine that you can ever actually rely on them.

ASSERTIVENESS

This is a good example of an 'irregular noun', in which the meaning changes with the subject, i.e., 'I express my beliefs honestly; you are assertive; he is insufferably dogmatic.'

Assertiveness is of limited value to the bluffer since you are probably less concerned about expressing your opinions than about hiding the fact that you do not have any.

Counter-assertiveness may be of more interest. When faced with one of those people who have been on assertiveness courses, and who thinks the way to control a meeting is to talk everyone else down, the trick is to let them drone on for a while. Then, when they are running out of steam, and everyone else in the meeting is getting a bit bored, hit them with your best point or the devastating question you have been saving up. Again, it all comes down to timing. Get it right and you can steal a meeting with a few words from a bore who has used thousands.

PLANNING

In the real world only proprietors or chief executives actually plan. Everyone else only imitates them, because even top managers generally work within guidelines laid down in tablets of stone from above (the boardroom, not heaven, although the former often confuses itself with the latter).

It follows that most managers and so-called planners are just monkeys, not organ grinders, usually plugging away within predetermined boundaries. Those who allege planning as a significant part of their contribution can be deflated by the same sort of question used to test candidates: 'What did you plan that actually came to fruition?' The follow-up question borders on the sadistic: 'What benefits resulted?' There is often a deafening silence.

The best posture where planning is concerned is to omit it from descriptions of your work while retaining the option to say or imply that, of course, planning is part of one's job but that, like breathing, it doesn't really need to be mentioned.

PRESENTING

Whether preparing a presentation, selling a project or just talking for the sake of it, do not forget the WWWWW (Who, What, When, Where, Why) acronym.

If you forget what it stands for, then try to remember Kipling's quotation from *The Elephant's Child*:

I keep six honest serving-men,
(They taught me all I knew);
Their names are What and Why and When
And How and Where and Who.

Thanks, Rudyard. Come to think of it, perhaps the acronym should be WWWHWW, but that does not really stick in the mind very well – which is the fate of most acronyms. Anyway, asking these questions may also aid your own understanding, which always helps.

MANAGING BY OBJECTIVE (MBO)

A splendid thing when done properly, this consists of identifying objectives in consultation with each job holder, for each job. You then have a yardstick against which to measure and assist the individual. Even if there is no formal MBO programme, you should be doing this within your own area of responsibility. It will help you to understand your subordinates' work, and help them to understand their responsibilities and the wider goals involved.

If by any chance you are the victim of a bad MBO programme, the things that make it bad will also enable you to discredit it. Almost certainly they will include:

a) failure to agree objectives with individuals

b) setting objectives late

c) setting unattainable objectives

d) confusing tasks with objectives

e) failure to monitor progress or discuss with staff

f) failure of your predecessor to do his/her job properly (the most popular explanation).

DELEGATION

Delegation is an absolute sine qua non for bluffing as it helps you to avoid having to do anything yourself. The best way to delegate work (D) is to list all your areas of responsibilities and break them down into chunks (C). Then look at the number of people available to you (N) and divide the chunks equally by said number, taking into consideration their ability, motivation and time. The formula may therefore be expressed as $C/N=D$.

Avoid the temptation to palm off the toughest tasks on the weakest subordinates – not out of altruism but because it is common sense. Ten to one the job will come back to you so badly done that you will have to do it all over again – and at short notice.

There is an old axiom: 'The world is divided into people who do things and people who take the credit.'

Get it right and this skill has many desirable results. Staff will thank you for giving them a more interesting and varied work plan and will become your most ardent supporters; and you will be amazed at how much work you (i.e., 'they') can accomplish. An increased perception of your management ability should follow,

There is an old axiom: 'The world is divided into people who do things and people who take the credit.' The latter have mastered the art of delegation. However, it is wise to remember that to be a good manager one is supposed to pass on the credit and praise when things go well, and accept all responsibility when they don't.

A little of the former will make you look like a jolly good sort, though there is no need to overdo it. A bit of the latter is also occasionally advisable, but only if you make it clear that you're doing the noble thing. And if your subordinates cock up in a big way, never, ever offer to fall on your sword. The offer might be accepted.

DECISION-MAKING

One of the problems about being a manager is that you are obliged to make decisions from time to time. This can be very troublesome and is well summed up by the old joke: 'He's known as Jigsaw because every time he's faced with a problem, he goes to pieces.'

But there is another, very helpful epigram which should be your watchword: 'If you can keep your head when all about you are losing theirs and blaming it on you, you'll be a manager, my son.'

The appearance of calm in a crisis is often indistinguishable from frozen panic. Both involve doing nothing, or at least as little as possible, in reaction to the crisis. You can justify this by mentioning the Kepner-Tregoe theory of problem analysis which suggests that you should not attempt any decisions until you have analysed the problem thoroughly. This is a valid excuse for never making any decision about anything.

The next line of defence is delegation. You can buy time and look very professional by delegating large areas of responsibility to subordinates on the basis that they need only consult you about exceptional cases. This is good management practice because people will rarely bother someone for a decision if it makes them look as if they don't know how to do their job.

And if the day should arrive when you are brought

the exceptional case, Plan A is to ask, 'What choices do you feel we have?' and then, 'Which would you recommend?' Half the time the person asking just wants you to ratify their decision for comfort or security. If he or she doesn't have a solution, Plan B is to find out how long you can defer the decision without adverse consequences, in the hope that when the time runs out the situation could have resolved itself.

Strange to say, it usually does.

RECRUITMENT

Many managers have little or no say in the selection of the people they end up managing. If, however, you have any control over recruitment, you should use that power to build up a team to whom you can safely delegate as much as possible. Your first decision when faced with a vacancy is to choose whether you want to fill the post or to eliminate it. If you eliminate the post, you save money, which will impress your superiors. If you fill the post, you will keep up the number of people under your authority, which will impress everyone else.

As a general rule, the number of people under a manager's authority is seen as a sign of that manager's virility (even when the manager is a woman) – the organisational equivalent of the deep croak of an alpha bullfrog or a peacock's tail spread out in a full mating display. In reality, there may be no correlation between the number of subordinates and power within the organisation – indeed, an executive with a tiny support staff, by having fewer people to manage, has more time to focus on building influence in the organisation – but perception is important and can often become reality.

Having lots of subordinates also means having more people to whom you can delegate your own work. Against that, the bluffer should remember that the more subordinates one has, the greater the responsibility and the more time one must spend managing them.

In the private sector, where money matters more, a small, tight team is usually the better option; in the public sector, where the perception of power is more important and money matters less, the optimal number of subordinates is often calculated using the well-known management scientific formula: 'the more, the merrier.'

Having decided to recruit, you need to define exactly what you want in a subordinate. Never mind the formal job specifications; here is what you really want from your new recruit:

1. evidence of dogged loyalty to previous managers

2. a capacity for prodigious hard work

3. limited ambition

4. low charisma (you don't want to be upstaged)

5. lack of guile (and thus evidence that the individual is not a fellow bluffer).

An extra filter is always helpful, whether it comes from your own team, boss, HR staff or an outside source.

That way, if the person turns out to be an unfortunate appointment, you can blame someone else.

COMMUNICATION

Communicating like a proper manager is not just about talking and using the right jargon, but also about listening. In fact, by making listening your craft, you can earn a fair amount of respect as a caring and thoughtful manager.

Even though you might think that you are doing a good job at communicating, you will probably find that your staff think they are being kept in the dark. A rule of thumb is to communicate three or four times more often than you think you need to so that each person is more likely to get the message.

One of the great frustrations of life in general, but especially life in management, is that you can repeat an instruction to someone until they get a bit impatient and say 'You don't need to keep telling me' – and, almost invariably, they will still get it wrong.

Getting a simple message across a large department accurately is in truth quite difficult. People read what they want to believe, hear what they want to hear, and generally behave like people who have not fully mastered English and do not plan to. The exceptions are often those to whom English really is a second language, who tend to be more exact about working out what words actually mean.

Good managers have every right to insist that presentations of all kinds, inside and outside the organisation, be presented in words of few syllables which a child of four could understand. If you can master the art of conveying information to other employees successfully, you are ahead of the game.

STAFF EMPOWERMENT

A couple of decades or so ago 'staff empowerment' became the vogue in the management world. Empowerment is linked closely with delegation, since it is about providing the opportunities for staff to take responsibility, share power and make decisions that not only benefit the business but also, and most importantly, benefit them. At least, that's the general idea.

Of course, no one actually meant it and one rarely hears the word 'empowerment' these days. Still, some of those involved in management theory look back on those days with nostalgia, in the same way that hippies look back on the Flower Power movement of the 1960s as a time of naïve hope and innocence.

(We were there, man. We were there.)

The concept remains useful to the bluffer as a pretext for the more radical forms of delegation; just do not expect your superiors to accept it as a valid excuse when things go wrong to say that 'I was empowering my people.' Saying it is one thing, but no hierarchy will tolerate the loss of control it implies in practice.

TIME MANAGEMENT

If you are to stand any chance of managing other people and resources, you must first learn to manage your own use of time. Good managers do this naturally, or through intense self-discipline. Bad managers never achieve it. They tend not to last.

To give a fair imitation of a good manager, try:

- minimising interruptions
- avoiding pointless meetings
- setting aside thinking time
- checking whether any suggested commitment has relevance to your objectives.

All this helps. The 'my-door-is-always-open' management style does not (not least because you may be interrupted when reading the latest copy of *Wisden* or doing a sudoku puzzle). Balancing the need for a good manager to be accessible with the need to do some things without distraction dictates that you be accessible at certain regular times, and only at those times, except in emergencies.

Identifying unmanaged time in others is simple: watch for the overtime epidemic. Managers who like overtime are highly suspect. Those who take work home are positively dangerous.

The irony is that long hours are inefficient. All the evidence suggests that time is used more productively, and better decisions made, by people who are well rested, well nourished, well exercised and who maintain a healthy work life balance.

If you find yourself in an organisation with a macho culture of being the last to leave the office, you might mention the Vickers studies, which demonstrated how, in less than a month, the productivity of overtime actually falls back to that of a standard working week.

If your hints go unnoticed, you might consider looking for a new organisation.

INNOVATION

If you are pedalling like mad to stay in the same place, the added strain of innovating products, services or internal systems and practices may not come easily. We have nothing against innovation. Someone has to do it. From time to time you may wish to try it for yourself. However, there is the 'better mousetrap' problem. It is truly said that if you build the better mousetrap the world will beat a path to your door, but most of us usually do not have the formula for a better mousetrap about our persons. Tactically, it may be better to approve wholeheartedly of the concept of innovation, but shuffle off to someone else the task of implementation. Or else be equipped with reasons for doing it later.

Millionaire innovators are often great self-publicists; what is less well publicised is how many great innovators died penniless. The millionaires tend to be the people who did it second, or third or tenth or eleventh, but did it properly. Few people know that a man called Woodruff invented the railway sleeping car – undeniably first, if not very good. So the Woodruff car is better known as the Pullman, after George Pullman – who did it later and better.

OPTIMISING PROFITABILITY

In a private sector organisation, the ability to optimise profitability is the way to the top. This can be done by increasing sales, decreasing costs or a combination of both.

In general, it is easier to reduce costs than to increase sales. However, it should never be forgotten that cutting costs may impact on the overall efficiency and profitability of the organisation. It is amazing how many 'efficiency reviews' conclude that the sales department is extravagant, with predictable results....

If your career development strategy is based solely on building a reputation as a cost-cutter, you must always make sure that you get your promotion and move on quickly before you have to deal with all the consequences of your actions.

When in doubt, get the number crunchers in; that is what they are there for. They love this stuff.

When no longer in doubt – because everything has gone wrong – blame the number crunchers.

EFFECTIVE PURCHASING/PROCUREMENT

Here is a great tip for the truly ambitious: take an active interest in the purchasing or procurement departments of a large organisation. They are often of immense significance to the organisation as a whole, especially in terms of costs, but they are often neglected by top management, who tend to be obsessed with more glamorous activities like marketing. Consider the example of Ernest Shackleton, the legendary polar explorer. He began his career as Third Officer on the Discovery expedition to the Antarctic led by Robert Falcon Scott in 1901 and was put in charge of holds, stores and provisions. This role sounds terribly dull, and hardly an effective use of his undoubted talents, but Shackleton quickly realised that a properly packed and well-balanced ship was pivotal to the success of the voyage. Popular with the crew, he quickly eclipsed the aloof and distant Scott and was widely regarded as a polar expedition leader in waiting. Why? Because he knew what was needed, how much it cost, and where it was all kept.

A manager who can take a firm grip of the process of buying the right goods at the right price at the right time can build a reputation as a cost-cutter and, at the same time, open up the organisation to new opportunities. Contact with buyers, and therefore with suppliers, gives an overview of the markets as a whole that may be lacking in more inward-looking departments. Buyers, or 'purchasing agents' in bluffer-speak, are the Cinderellas of most organisations; they often feel under-appreciated but they are important players, especially if they also get involved in marketing, as in some retail operations. This gives them the chance to get it right at both ends. Or wrong.

It is not necessary to know too much about buying except that if the staff hold their positions uncomplainingly for too long they are likely to be:

a) complacent about new suppliers
b) undermotivated
c) on the fiddle
d) all three.

Be nice to them and see what happens.

EFFECTIVE MANAGEMENT OF FINANCES

Good phrases for a bluffer to use when presented with masses of incomprehensible figures are, 'Do you really believe the bottom-line effect?' and, 'Do you think it is meaningful to ignore overhead allocation?' This is effective whether they do or not. Their answers (in the unlikely event that they know what you are talking about) will tell you which position they are defending. The real killer is: 'Can you simplify this so that the board would understand?'

You may also be faced with:

- **management accounts** which, because they are generated by accountants, are seldom wholly or even partially intelligible to management

- **cost accounts** which mean roughly what they say

- **financial accounts** which lead up to the 'statutories' in the annual report.

Acceptable matters for debate when discussing any of these include the extent to which they are integrated with each other. In theory, they ought to be. In practice, there are gaps or gulfs of which accountants in particular are well aware. You can usefully ask: 'How much could this change in the final figures?' The only telling response would be, 'These are the final figures', which you may counter with the definitive low blow: 'There is never a final figure.' This is true, even when the company is insolvent and being wound up.

WE'LL MEET AGAIN (AND AGAIN)

HOLDING EFFECTIVE MEETINGS

It is said that managers only have meetings when they don't know what to do. This is not wholly true. Managers also have them when they do know what to do, but don't want to do it; or want someone else to do it; or want the blame spread a bit if everything goes wrong. Meetings are rarely popular and most participants will begrudge the time wasted, which gives you an excellent opportunity to score heavily by conducting the perfect meeting: a short one.

All meetings should have an objective. It is good practice to send out an agenda and to get people on your side at the start by eliciting their input for agenda items. When planning the meeting, don't just seek an outcome; have your own in mind before you start (a quick and merciful conclusion is a good one). You can even write the desired minutes in advance and then steer the meeting round to the course you recommend. This is as 'democratic' as anything in ancient or modern Greek practice, and rather more fun. Above all, you must manage the process of the meeting and keep it moving at a brisk pace.

It is important to nail down all decisions and actions for attendees, so record the decisions yourself. Remember that Stalin rose to power by taking on the thankless task of Secretary of the Central Committee of the Communist Party. He understood that what matters at a meeting matters less than what the minutes say happened. So 'Comrade Stalin was censured' could somehow get typed up as, 'Comrade Stalin was congratulated on being given supreme executive power.'

'Your top of the funnel content must be intellectually divorced from your product but emotionally wed to it.'
Digital Leader at InsightSquared.

HOLDING INEFFECTIVE CONTENT HUDDLES

In every management environment there are professional meeting holders. These are managers who spend their entire working lives sitting around a table exhaling Hindenburg quantities of hot air (or hydrogen). It is as if they have no purpose outside a meeting, and you might reasonably wonder where they find the time to actually do their jobs. The answer is that holding meetings *is* their job. Bluffers must strive to avoid meeting 'invitations' from these people, not least because they will monopolise your time, make your job more difficult, and add significantly to the backlog of work you haven't quite got round to. And don't overlook the fact that they are experts in what they do, because it is all that they do. It gives them a profound sense of self-worth. Wherever possible, delegate attendance to hapless juniors (but don't expect them to come back undamaged).

The worst offender is our new young friend the director of digital strategy (see page 23). The DDS has carte blanche to examine any area of the business which he feels might benefit from his laser-like digital insight. Don't underestimate him (and it is nearly always a him). He might look as though he's only 23, but he could be 31, 40 or even 12. In most instances he has been parachuted in by a black-ops team from LinkedIn, armed with the existential brief of something like 'reinvigorating the brand'. But the newly empowered strategy wunderkind has more sinister motives. He is on a mission to trample over as many people as he can in his quest to acquire ever more board-level acronyms to paper over the cracks of his suspiciously confident LinkedIn profile. The most effective DDS can slither expertly and almost without notice into the higher echelons of the company hierarchy. This is because he is fluent in every aspect of the language of the intricately programmed media age digibot, and nobody else dares to admit they're still muddling along at Janet & John Level One Digital Esperanto.

The truly effective bluffer needs a – you've guessed it – strategy, to draw the sting from the DDS's shiny new digital lexicon. If you still have a modern management rulebook in your head, instead of an app that's going to change the world within the next ten minutes, then it's time to rip it up. Let's just tell it how it is: it's jargon not a lexicon. There's no point dressing these things up. Bluffers should, however, verse themselves in the verbiage of a new and constantly evolving lingua franca for digital strategy meetings. But hold this thought tighter than a Hoxton hipster's grip on his smartphone at a moped convention: management speak in the age of social media domination has gone through a lightning-quick paradigm shift, particularly in the mystifying set-piece of the strategy meeting. These have careered off in a major digital detour since blue-sky thinking, backburners and running such-and-such up flagpoles induced myriad Reggie Perrin moments in offices of the recent past.

It's no longer effective enough merely to wax away in corporate bingo-lingo as charmingly old-fashioned as 'touching base', or 'dialling in for a conference call'. Thanks to the emergence of a successful and unstoppable breeding programme of digital strategists in the corporate incubator, the modern management bluffer must reinvent his and her metaphors, digitise the wheel by cross-pollinating that tired old invention for the 21st century consumer lifecycle, and ingest a whole new language.

First of all, you'll need to be prepared to go 'granular' with your belief systems. And, time permitting, in what everyone claims is a 'time-poor digital environment', be ever mindful of the conversion rates of your segmented demographic. Before you know it you'll be laughing along with the rest of the digital disciples (through gritted teeth).

The natural arena in which the digital strategy expert chooses to showcase his thought-leadership prowess is the gladiatorial setting of the 'content huddle'. Note to bluffers: in a blindingly enlightened management masterstroke, digital strategy huddles should be at the very least two hours long and routinely scheduled for 9am on a Monday morning, just to ensure everyone's chasing their tails catching up on answering/deleting emails (in no particular order) for the rest of the working week. Attendees should, too, make sure that they are sitting round the meeting table, calm, prompt, and fully prepared by bang on said 9am, ready for the arrival, to the second, of The Strategist. None of that bowling in, all flustered, at two minutes past with hastily spilt coffees and lame excuses. Digital strategy isn't just digital strategy, however you might read it. It is Year Zero business management. And there will be another digital strategy content huddle tomorrow. And again this afternoon until close of play if this strategy thing is really going to sprout wings. Bluffers should not be tempted to point out that they actually have a full-time job doing something else. If they make this critical mistake, the cold, dead, unblinking eye of the strategy necromancer will settle upon them and their days might well be numbered (depending on their management level). Bite your tongue and look enthused, in the hope and expectation that the DDS will at some stage move on to another area of the business, taking his penetrating exposition of the digital realm with him.

In the wearisome linguistic melee of the content huddle it's important – and, remember, when navigating the rich media environment of the global digi-scape *everything* is *important*, if not *super-important* – for the switched-on digital bluffer to be expertly versed in tech business news and trends from about an hour ago, max. If you haven't got a clue what game-changing trends in the field of search engine optimisation were emerging from Palo Alto, California, within the past 60 minutes, because you live in Bexleyheath, skipped breakfast and had a bus to catch, bluff things out with a fleeting tech insight from Google published only ten minutes ago. Play it right, and you'll be tasked by the DDS to action your learnings and findings into a set of fully costed, end-user deliverables overnight.

But enter the digital strategy meeting unprepared at your peril. The strategist has been expertly wired by the web development team to spot whether or not you are as fully responsive to content marketing silos and brand dialogue behaviours as anyone pretending to have a proper job should be. This is where the bluffer can nod and assiduously note-take, ready to use those terms with a knowledgeable flourish at the next digital strategy meeting, due to start in an hour's time.

If you do take the risk of simply winging it, the ill-versed bluffer can expect to feel stricken throughout those soul-sapping hours in the fetid air of the meeting room by nagging, nervy waves of FOMO (Fear of Missing

Out) or even FOBFO (Fear of Being Found Out). If all else fails, at this point bluffers should put on their 'this meeting is super-important' face. There might be an app for it you can download on most networks..

Bluffers should take careful note of the following *#winning* suite of wide-ranging digital realignments (and bumper on-the-spot tips for re-engineering the business process while you're at it) and use them liberally in strategy content huddles. This way, you will be guaranteed to boost your customer-facing throughput and gain best-practice insights into behavioural targeting, all the while fostering those lovely, warm, inner feelings of core competency that we all cherish. Clear on that?

'A child of five would understand this. Send someone to fetch a child of five.'

Groucho Marx

MUSCULAR MANAGEMENT

Be combative. This isn't a digital strategy meeting: it's a fight. A fight without fists over who's got the biggest brain and best thoughts; who's tooled up with the toughest virtual axe to chip hard at the base rock of the cyber coalface and reveal the lucrative deposits below. Imagine Oliver Reed and Alan Bates wrestling in a barn in *Women In Love*, not over a comely maiden but over an iPhone X – forever – and you'll emerge from the meeting chest-puffed, head-high and ready to prioritise a blizzard of action points.

GRAINS OF TRUTH

Granularity – or going granular – is a double-edged sword of a mixed metaphor on the DDS's home turf of a strategy meeting. Therefore, it's wise for the bluffer on the receiving end to tread carefully. Granularity is a digital content sidekick of *drilling down*, and a bluffer can either get 'too granular' in deeply analysing the likes of webpages and how many people are looking at them or – perhaps – not. But not being granular enough could in turn lead to further unwanted delegation of duties to the unwary.

SEXY CONTENT

No, not that sort of website. The quest for 'sexy content', which is basically stuff that's useful, interesting and which a human being might be reasonably expected to read for more than a few seconds, should be an occasional reference point for a bluffer leading a digital strategy meeting (keen bluffers might like 'to benchmark' this now). Expect a couple of funny looks and sniggers at the back.

EMOTIONAL CONTENT

A platonic friend of sexy content, this is content that's both action and thought-provoking which can drive you to share, to like, to comment and – that word again – engage. But emotional content is definitely something the bluffer should mention. Add to that an earnest platitude such as 'emotion should inform all our content' and – bingo! – the punters might actually increase their 'dwell time' (*see* Glossary) while they're in such a fragile online state.

THE VERTICAL CHALLENGE

This is the how-and-the-where of structural parts of a website, where different topics, subject matter, sections, subsections and all that jazz are categorised – sometimes even correctly. Here, these noble verticals can stand tall and proud within the 'information architecture' (the way it's set up and that) of said site. A bluffer should empower his or her digital team members to 'own' a vertical. Or two if they're lucky. That doesn't mean you can take it home for the weekend like the primary school hamster, but you should feed it with rich and engaging content while in the office nonetheless.

STAIRCASE TO (REVENUE) HEAVEN

Readers of a certain vintage might have heard of strategic staircases. A lot of people hid under them during the Blitz. Nowadays, since the end of Luftwaffe carpet bombing of British towns and cities their digital strategy descendants have innovatively managed to reinvent the staircase as a long-term revenue-boosting tool for successful business growth. The idea is that, over time, people who look at your digital wares eventually start buying, or at least buying in to, stuff. Staircase your strategy correctly, and you might actually sell something.

THE WHITEBOARD JUNGLE

It's a big fat myth that all things digital have taken over the corporate world. There's still a refreshingly analogue style that even the most switched-on management bluffers might like to adopt, when they are feeling particularly corporately empowered to deliver deliverables in a team briefing meeting setting. The humble whiteboard, complete with colourful marker pens, can add delightful retro-fit stylings to the grey of a post-PowerPoint world. Some of the assembled throng can be invited up to the whiteboard, too, to brainstorm some verticals and get those Venn diagrams working harder for their keep.

END-TO-END STUFF

It has been known for a bluffer to evangelise about the online user journey process – or end-to-end fulfilment – as 'from pulpit to conversion'. Bolder bluffers might do well to follow this example and delve into a digital Damascus as they dip their toes in the font of such enlightening consumer insights, chanting the mantra 'Ocado' as they take the glorious path to customer fulfilment which only total digital conversion can bring.

FUN

After five straight working days of finding out loads of exciting brand-new digital strategy things, what's end-of-week catnip to the content huddlers as the clock inches towards 5pm on Friday? How about a Friday afternoon quiz at 5.01pm, where you can all be tested on the digital insights, learnings and deliverables of the week in a relaxed office environment? This is enlightened touchy-feely management as practised by self-aggrandising flunkies who have absolutely no concept of a life outside the corporate bubble. Make your excuses and run for the hills before you're asked if you might like to task the team with extra learnings and analytics as weekend homework, ready for Monday's 9am sharp content huddle – including individual 20-minute presentations. So, you see, it's not all work work work. Except for all-day Sunday.

The best way to lose demotivated incompetents may be to recommend them for promotion. You would be amazed by how many glittering management careers started this way.

TOOLS OF THE TRADE

There are many management 'tools' in use today, with more coming all the time. The bluffer does not need to use them all, but you do need to be aware of them. You may find that instructing your staff in these techniques is an excellent way to appear wise and clever.

THE VISION STATEMENT

A vision statement is a declaration of intent regarding where you want your business to get to within a certain timeframe. Some of them can be rather ambitious, even fanciful. For example, if you are in the business of mousetrap manufacture, it could say: 'Our company is going to be the best rodent exterminator in this country within five years.'

The idea of the 'vision' is that it allows a team to believe in a higher purpose (especially if there isn't one). The essentials of a vision statement are:

- who you are (subject)
- where you are going (purpose)
- what will drive the behaviour of the business (values).

Some organisations have a separate 'values statement' as well as, or instead of, the vision statement. The statement, whatever it is called, needs to be clear so that everyone can easily understand it. This means it should be as short as possible. You then need to use it frequently, quoting it as a pretext for your more inexplicable decisions. Getting the vision statement right has the result of instantly promoting you to visionary leader status. Getting it wrong will make you the object of mockery.

At the back of many a stationery cupboard and in the corner of many a warehouse is a dusty pile of unread copies of some glorious vision statement or statement of values that was soon overtaken by events in the real world and subsequently forgotten.

THE MISSION STATEMENT

A good mission statement can give focus to your efforts and those of your staff. To do that, it needs above all to be short – so that people actually remember it. It should be no more than one sentence, pithily summing up what your organisation – or your bit of the organisation – exists to do and why. For example, if the business is about making mousetraps, the mission statement might say: 'We make traps that dispatch mice by humane and environmentally friendly means.'

It's an excellent tool for bluffers because memorising and reiterating the simple statement makes you sound like an authority on the business.

THE BUSINESS PLAN

The business plan exists to turn the mission statement into reality. Where the mission statement gives a general direction, the plan is the roadmap to get there. It sets specific objectives, usually with quantifiable targets as milestones along the way. It then describes the strategy by which those objectives are to be reached and, most importantly, how much it will cost.

If you are charged with drafting such a plan and then implementing it you should seek to make the targets as achievable as corporate politics permit. Set them low so you get credit by exceeding them as much as possible.

Alternatively, set impressive targets and move on before you have to reach them.

BENCHMARKING

If you want to impress your colleagues with your skills in total quality management, then a good tool to know about and to encourage others to use is benchmarking. Xerox first adopted this practice – so no surprise that other companies just can't help copying it.

Benchmarking is used to improve business performance and should lead to the adoption of best practice by the simple expedient of emulating the way 'best-in-class' companies do things. It is a good idea to measure your outfit against the highest-performing organisation that you can find.

To fit in with the TQM approach, benchmarking should be used on a continuous basis and should result in the evaluation of current business practice with the aim of achieving excellence. There is a range of different types of benchmarking – for example, competitive, strategic, process, product, customer service, internal etc. All approaches are designed to compare your products, services and practices against those of world-class competitors.

The hotshot manager will know that the most important part of benchmarking is what the organisation does after the exercise is over.

BRAINSTORMING

Brainstorming, also now known as 'Thought Showering', is an effective method for using teams to develop potential solutions to questions or problems. At the beginning of a brainstorming session, everyone needs to understand the central question, after which the discussion must be steered in such a way that everyone has an opportunity to speak and contribute to the generation of ideas. Every idea must be recorded (however daft this might sound), and only when the flow of ideas has dried up should a halt be called to the meeting.

This should appeal to the bluffer, since it removes the obligation for you to come up with any ideas of your own. You should offer to 'facilitate', i.e., chair the meeting, so that you are able to sit there, nodding benignly, as though you had already thought of all these ideas yourself and are just letting everyone else have their say.

OUTSOURCING

Benchmarking not only allows you to compare how your organisation shapes up to the best; it also shows where it may be more cost-efficient to outsource specific parts of the business to other organisations that can do the job better, faster and cheaper. It is difficult for any business to be world class in every aspect, so concentrate your resources on the organisation's key competences and leave the other tasks to external agencies.

Many organisations have been able to cut costs by 30% to 40% by outsourcing. Bluffers may even think of doing this 100%, and offshore, except that it tends to attract unkind media comment.

TEAMBUILDING

Although teambuilding is an achingly trendy subject, resist the temptation to mock it. Having an effective team means that you can delegate large amounts of your work, which is the bluffer's ultimate goal. To achieve it, you need to choose carefully to get the right mix of people, and you need to be certain that each has the skills to accomplish the necessary tasks.

Putting the right people on the right teams can be very effective. They can be used as think tanks to solve problems and to generate the new ideas that most bluffers could never generate on their own. They can also source information that you didn't know was needed, for which of course you will be able to take overall credit. Note the word 'overall'. The canny bluffer will avoid taking direct credit but will always make a point of going overboard to praise 'my team'. The great advantage of this is that you can say things about your team that would seem immodest if you said them about yourself.

When you form a team, be clear about what you expect to be accomplished and talk about how you envisage those involved working together. It is more than a matter of putting the same sort of people together. Teams, like marriages, work best where there are differences as well as similarities; no human being is perfect so it helps when one's own weaknesses are covered by someone else's strengths, and vice versa. It is also a bad idea to have a team consisting only of high achievers; there is only room for one big ego per team.

There is a ton of literature on the psychology of teams and the various social roles that are said to exist within the most successful of them. You need not go into too much detail because everyone has their own favourite set of labels and is unfamiliar with everyone else's. Just develop a homely analogy of your own like, 'I love tomatoes but you need more than tomatoes to make a salad.'

Finally, remember that building the team is only the beginning. You have to lead it. It might be helpful to think of team development in four stages: Forming, Storming, Norming and Performing:

Forming *Selection*
Storming *Brainstorming*
Norming *Sorting the realistic from the eccentric*
Performing *Actual work*

(Unfortunately, FSNP isn't a very helpful acronym, so just try to remember the Storming Norming bits.)

MEASURING STAFF PERFORMANCE

Research has shown that the most influential thing about productivity is gaining feedback on people's performance. In simple terms, this just means letting staff know how they are doing, and also how they are doing compared with their colleagues. It also means letting them know that their superiors are keeping an eye on them.

The methods for measuring staff performance vary greatly from organisation to organisation and come under many guises, from the plain-old 'appraisal' to 'performance monitoring' to much more grand schemes such as 'performance management and development programme'. Essentially, the objective is about how to motivate behaviour and generate continuous improvement.

Here are the best-known methods of measuring staff performance, which if dropped into conversation with any HR manager will generally produce a warm glow:

360-degree approach

This performance appraisal uses feedback received from a variety of sources, including one's colleagues, from managers and even from the people one is in contact with during normal business time. An all-round view of this kind does not necessarily generate kindly comment. It's a bit like the condemned being asked to pass an opinion on the police, the prosecuting counsel and the judge.

Situational leadership approach

A terrific-sounding management tool for bluffers. Basically, in appraising performance, the approach focuses on an individual's competence and commitment – two very different things.

In an ideal world, every post would be filled with people who are both competent and committed. This is not an ideal world.

Competence is a function of knowledge and skills and can be gained through education, training and experience. Commitment is a function of confidence and motivation. In an ideal world, every post would be filled with people who are both competent and committed. This is not an ideal world. One often encounters a competent employee working at half-speed due to a lack of motivation. Less frequent, but still not uncommon, is the employee who is keen to get on but sadly not up to the job. It is hard to say which has the potential to do most damage.

Your job is to fit the people you have available into the positions you need to fill. Do your best to improve both competence and motivation but accept that you are not going to turn every one of your subordinates into the ideal. If someone is lacking in either, put them in a position where they can do least harm; if they lack both, get rid of them.

The best way to get rid of the useless is to fire them,

but this is not always easy – for one thing, bluffers in particular are tender-hearted folk, tolerant of the weaknesses of others because we are aware of the weaknesses in ourselves.

The alternative is to transfer them to another department, but your peers are probably on guard – as you should be – against unsolicited lateral transfers of the unwanted.

So the best way to lose demotivated incompetents may be to recommend them for promotion. You would be amazed by how many glittering management careers started this way…or maybe you would not be surprised at all.

SMART WORKING

You can apply Smart working to setting strategic, personal and staff objectives. The purpose is to set specific, measurable, attainable, relevant and trackable goals:

Specific The objectives should state what the desired outcome is, or what the person is responsible for.

Measurable There is a need to state how the progress or performance is going to be measured.

Attainable The objectives and goals need to be realistic and reasonable.

Relevant It has to be remembered that 80% of performance comes from 20% of tasks.

Trackable It is vital to monitor progress against time.

Use of the Smart route allows you to set realistic targets and at the same time allows you to keep track of all progress being made. This is a particularly useful approach in that you can coach or support as necessary. The sleight of hand in setting objectives is to get your subordinates to write their own. All you then need to do is check that they are Smart – job done.

STAFF TRAINING

Training is very much in vogue. A lot of organisations like to boast of their investment in their people, and managers who are seen to take it seriously do their careers no harm.

The problem is that there are a vast number of courses on offer and they vary enormously in quality. The best are life-changing and increase the value of any participant as an asset to their organisation. But many – perhaps most – are cash cows for colleges or dodgy training companies that restate the obvious and leave the participant with no more than a meaningless certificate. How can an innocent manager pick the ones that might actually do some good?

The trick here is similar to objective setting; get your staff to research training options themselves and then present their recommendations to you. Make it clear beforehand that budgets and common sense may not stretch to all the suggestions being made. Especially if they involve foreign travel – unless of course they are management-level courses, in which case you might consider leading from the front and showing your personal commitment to constant training and refreshment of your own skills.

BUSINESS PROCESS RE-ENGINEERING

Another superb tool in the bluffer's metaphorical shed, this involves the drastic redesign of core business processes to achieve significant changes in productivity, efficiency and quality. The process typically focuses on delivering added value to the customer (meaning something extra and nice which they might not have been expecting). Cynics say that business process re-engineering is more about finding a new name for something that has been happening for years.

FLOWCHARTING

Flowcharts are a good device to represent and communicate complex processes that would otherwise involve considerable effort to document. They are also meant to be useful for demonstrating to other managers and staff what exactly is supposed to be going on. But this is wishful thinking. Nobody really understands them.

What could be more perfect for the bluffer? You could even invent new symbols: a flower shape would be nice.

BUDGETING

A budget is a statement of the expenditure and/or income of the business for a set period of time. This is a management tool with which most managers purport to control their areas of responsibility. The budget specifies for the future period the costs, expenses and revenues forecast to arise for a 'profit centre', which may be a complete business or a discrete section of one.

For the new manager, the difficulty is that you tend to inherit someone else's budget (invariably overspent), taking over midstream when things are even more incomprehensible than they might otherwise be.

Two of the common approaches are the 'incremental budget' and the 'zero-based budget' (both useful for bluffers). The incremental budget is based on using last year's figures. The budget is based on how the last year went, plus or minus an adjustment to take things like inflation into account. NB: it tends to take for granted things that have ceased and fails to consider changes during the period. In other words, it is fiction.

The zero-based budget is one in which you begin from scratch and analyse the cost from afresh at the start of the year, i.e., you develop the forthcoming year's budget without reference to last year's actual budget or costs. For this approach you will need to redefine objectives and also provide evidence to justify every item you include. Very easy to miss things, too.

When deciding which to use, you need to be realistic and not over-optimistic. It is also important that you do not do this in your own 'budget bubble' (remember this one). Be sure to involve others and also be sure that you don't leave too little time to complete the exercise. You can take it for granted that the new figures are likely to be better than the old. Traditional budget reviews are much too pedestrian to generate positive thoughts. They are usually concerned with preserving the status quo – plus or minus 10%.

BALANCE SHEETS

The balance sheet is a financial statement of the company assets and liabilities on a given date. A company may produce a balance sheet on any day for its own internal purposes, but one must be produced on the last day of the financial year for statutory purposes. This is often when managers, like sheets, are hung out to dry.

The balance sheet is a useful aid for the manager because a current version can be compared with a previous balance sheet to provide an indication of how the company is progressing (or not). The problem is that it is based on notional values – e.g., whether what one paid, one would have to pay now, or what one would sell for – with big differences between them. We are clearly back in the realm of fiction.

RETURN ON INVESTMENT

A useful yardstick for gauging the performance of a business (or a profit centre), this is an excellent measure to use on areas that report to you, but not so much fun when used against you (in which case you claim that your own little pocket is crucial and should not be assessed out of context).

The problem is that all the fixed assets and working capital which look so necessary when considered in isolation suddenly ruin your relative performance because every excess pound you are using shaves more off your effective return. All those uncollected debts, all the raw materials, work in progress, finished goods and stock in transit hither or thither cost money and depress the return. ROI provides a good incentive to reduce any and all of them.

SWOT ANALYSIS

This is a helpful aid when you are developing your strategic management plan. SWOT analysis requires you to identify the internal Strengths and Weaknesses of your business as well as the Opportunities and Threats to your organisation in the external business environment. This sounds simple because it is simple – but it can generate lists that run to several pages without telling you anything you did not know before. It is therefore a valuable tool for the bluffer. It is also a helpful acronym to drop into conversation whenever discussing strategy. Which, hopefully, will not be too often.

PEST ANALYSIS

Another satisfying acronym for bluffers with memory problems. This one is all about the pace of change and how coping with a constantly evolving external environment is a major challenge for managers. PEST analysis is therefore a useful and simple tool that can be used to track environmental impact on a business. It involves identifying the Political, Economic, Social and Technological influences on the organisation. It will be difficult for others to resist comparison with a) the weird guy from Systems with wandering hands and b) vermin to be eliminated.

In practice, PEST analysis involves little more than keeping an eye on the newspapers, but it can be made to look and sound very impressive.

CUSTOMER SATISFACTION SURVEY

The classic way to monitor how customers feel about your current level of service or the quality of your products is to carry out a customer satisfaction consultation. This is generally done by asking them questions. Here, you may wish to engage your market research unit or perhaps see it as a good opportunity to explore the use of external consultants. That way you can brand the results of the consultation as 'independent', and any criticism for unfavourable results can be attributed to the approach adopted by them.

The real value of such surveys is limited. They usually ask people to give detailed thought, at very short notice, to something they have never really bothered about. Do not expect anything profound.

You should only commission a survey when you have a point to make and you are fairly confident that the survey will support that point. Never rely on your customers to make your decision for you. They have no responsibility for the consequences of what they say. You do.

Again, remember the old trial lawyer's maxim: never ask anyone a question unless you know what their answer will be.

———————— *ℬ̈* ————————

As a bluffer, you might find a consultant rather convenient – someone who can actually do the management for you. It not only works quite effectively but also helps you to learn from a master bluffer…

OUTSIDE THE BOX

All enterprises will at some time have to rely on the advice and services of people outside the business, whose principal function is either:

1. to tell you something that you do not already know

2. to provide something that you do not already have (like money, staff or more customers)

3. to take the blame when things go wrong.

CONSULTANTS

Businesses are increasingly using consultants in every functional area. Their role is to deliver specialist skills from outside the organisation, supposedly. If you need help in any aspect of your business then it's a certain bet that there is a management consultant hanging around in reception who can help. As a bluffer, you might find a consultant rather convenient – someone who can actually do the management for you. It not only works quite effectively but also helps you to learn from a master bluffer...

...Which is of course the problem. Consultancy is an occupation that attracts more than its share of charlatans. Even the good ones may overcharge and may waste a lot of time 'learning about your business' (which you are paying for). You could end up with results that are of no use at all and a long, wordy, vague report that requires a PhD in cryptology to decipher.

Hiring the right sort of consultant is still the solution to a lot of problems, and usually a better option than hiring new staff on permanent contract, with all the legal and administrative hassle that entails. You just have to keep your consultant on a tight rein. Define exactly what you want, and then get the consultant to repeat it back to you very slowly so you can be sure that you are understood. Do not allow consultants to go wandering off, giving you what they think you need rather than what you want. This is what they like to do. Your job is to keep them on track.

BANKERS

Treat with caution. There are only two golden rules:

1. When things are going well and they notice enough to say so, ask them for something. More than you need.

2. When things are going badly, don't ignore them. Tell them how things are and when they might get

better. If possible, deliver the improvements earlier or better than forecast. This helps them to look good with their area or regional directors.

Bankers are very simple organisms, really, and quite Pavlovian in their reactions. If you have the opportunity you should befriend an optimist in your bank (rare, but they do exist). He/she will eventually get fired or demoted but in the meantime they're worth their weight in gold, possibly literally.

UNIONS

Unions only exist because of past management failures and weaknesses. Making union involvement less necessary is a laudable desire because its achievement will only flow from good employee relations. This is not in the unions' long-term interests, so do not expect them to help you. Never underestimate them. Union leaders are the winners in a Darwinian struggle for survival that makes management itself look tame.

Labour relations are best left to specialists. If you imagine that a bit of mutual goodwill, a bit of common sense, and a bit of give and take are all that's required for everyone to get along, then you have no place talking directly with union officials.

HEADHUNTERS

Obviously not small gentlemen with acute cannibalistic tendencies. The alternative name is 'search consultants' and only some of them have bones through their noses. To a headhunter, any manager is a potential candidate, client and source of information. It is often difficult to tell which way they want to use you because UK law makes it actionable to seduce someone away from his or her contracted employment. Headhunters therefore employ a contorted form of approach in which they appear to treat both sources and candidates identically, as sources of advice about a current vacancy. Think of the mating dance of scorpions. The convention is that if you are interested, you take the initiative and mention yourself. Alas, many people do not understand the convention and mention other people instead.

Some headhunters are suspected of industrial espionage. Others are suspected of acting for employers trying to test employee loyalty (or erode it). If on the receiving end, it is always advisable to affect disinterest at the first approach, and then check them out thoroughly. And ask yourself one question: if they were any good at their jobs, wouldn't they have rumbled you as a bluffer?

JOURNALISTS

Journalists don't have much to contribute to management but you need to watch the press to see what public opinion will do. In business at least the press form, rather than follow, public opinion. A bad story about a company may have no real basis in fact but it will still shake market confidence and so it will become fact.

If dealing with the media is unavoidable, just remember these guidelines:

a) Nominate one person in the organisation to deal with press enquiries. If things are going well one might nominate oneself; if things look more dubious, then nominate someone expendable.

b) Present the constructive side of things and never mention the downside, unless you can offer specific and credible contradiction.

c) Brief them about the company when things are quiet so that they have accurate background rather than collecting data against time later.

d) Mistrust them at all times.

Try to avoid saying 'no comment', which always seems shifty, but always have a few lines prepared in advance that mean the same thing – such as, 'We will be making a full statement shortly', i.e. before the end of the decade, assuming that everyone has not forgotten this whole unfortunate business by then. Where possible, distract their attention, ideally with another story. Journalists are a bit like infants; they can be quite obsessive about something that interests them – until something brighter and shinier comes along.

Feel free to take a metaphorical shredder to most areas of management literature, especially 'new management theory'.

GURUS AND THEORIES

Far too much is written far too seriously about management. You can be reassured that no one has ever read it all. Better still, all management literature is biodegradable, so feel free to take a metaphorical shredder to most areas of management literature, especially 'new management theory'.

It is not necessary to be intimate with each new idea. You need only know its name, then take evasive action as follows:

Phase 1 Call it 'a nine-day wonder'. If the new concept proves more permanent than that, proceed to:

Phase 2 In which you retain an open mind because 'it hasn't yet been validated'. If and when it receives acceptable initial validation, retreat to:

Phase 3 The stance that it requires large-scale practical examples of its worth over a realistic period. A 'realistic period', when you are on the defensive, means years, not months or weeks. From this position go on to:

Phase 4 Which consists of finding out more about the theory, once it has demonstrated its durability. Or, if that seems too much like hard work, claim it is out of date.

Happily, Phase 4 is rarely an issue because few new management theories survive that long in the real world.

GURUS AND GOOD NAMES

It is indeed strange that the word 'guru' is applied to the most successful management theorists. After all, the original gurus were Indian ascetics who renounced all worldly possessions. Modern gurus, on the other hand, take an obsessive interest in worldly possessions. Many of them, however, are Indian.

Management gurus are the rock stars of the management world. Some can command fees in excess of $100,000 for a single appearance. However, gurus come and go, so be aware of the pitfalls of gurudom. Those who stay tend to do so on the strength of their entertainment value, rather than their contribution to management theory and practice.

It is often difficult to differentiate a world-changing new management idea from a passing fad. So the safest option is to focus on those that have stood the test of time. The key to the future is usually in the past – which is the sort of thing a guru might say and get paid well for doing so.

Here are some of the names that it is safe to drop:

Peter Drucker

This is the name to remember if you forget everything else. You can safely preface any well-worn business cliché with 'Well, Drucker said...' – because he probably did. Drucker is considered to be the most influential management guru of all time and is the source of much of today's management theory. He was not only responsible for transforming management practice into a highly regarded discipline, he also had the uncanny ability to spot future trends in industry. He is given credit for the concept of the 'knowledge economy'.

Peter Drucker is the name to remember... You can safely preface any well-worn business cliché with 'Well, Drucker said...' – because he probably did.

If you need to remember a few soundbites, then try the two cornerstones of his work, *The Practice of Management* (1954) and *Management: Tasks, Responsibilities, Practices* (1973) – he was writing in the days before catchy titles became obligatory. However, Drucker has written so much over such a long period that it is not obligatory to remember any one chunk of it. The correct posture is to imply that you have absorbed it all so deeply that you have forgotten precise references. This device is made easier because Drucker lived in the real world and did not need to hang catchy labels on pet theories in order to be remembered.

Michael Porter

Porter is a Professor at Harvard Business School, which you can mention with respect or with contempt according to circumstance. The bluffer who lacks an MBA talking to a fellow non-MBA may find it useful to dismiss the 'academic theorising' of business schools, but whether one is for them or against them, there is no denying that Harvard is the most prestigious of them.

Porter's influence in the management field has been through the production of models of competitiveness for all levels of business. His main focus is on strategy and in particular the relationship between the strategy of the organisation and industry structure as a whole.

He is also the first management guru to refer to himself as a brand.

Tom Peters

Peters launched himself into management guru status with his book *In Search of Excellence* (1982). He co-wrote it with a chap called Robert Waterman, but it was Peters who transformed the selling of business ideas into an art form. However, he is renowned for a no-nonsense approach to addressing the business world and has also earned a reputation as the anti-guru guru.

Charles Handy

A UK-based Irishman, Handy can be regarded as the social conscience of management theory, with his first book *Understanding Organisations* (1976) starting to explore the social and philosophical aspects of management that can be observed in his later work. Unlike most who explore the touchy-feely aspects of management, he has a solid business background and his feet are firmly on the ground. He is one of the more readable gurus.

Gary Hamel

Hamel can be regarded as the voice of modern strategy, and his big hit was *Leading the Revolution* (2000). His main bone of contention is that there is an epidemic of complacency and cynicism in business, for which an antidote must be sought – a statement of the obvious if ever there was one, but he expressed it better. With C.K. Prahalad, he is the originator of the concept of 'core competences' which can be transferred from one activity to another – like bluffing.

Philip Kotler

Kotler is one of the world's leading experts on marketing, whose approach can be summed up in a famous quote – famous among management geeks anyway – 'Good companies will meet needs; great companies will create markets.' Despite his undoubted expertise in marketing, the best title he could come up with for his classic work was *Marketing Management: Analysis, Planning, Implementation and Control* (1993). This just proves that marketing and selling can be two very different things.

Henry Mintzberg

A slightly subversive Canadian, best known for his classification of different types of organisation, you might find Mintzberg useful to quote as a distinguished academic who has been very critical of the academic approach to management education. The title of his best-known work, *Managers Not MBAs* (2004), says it all. The title of his other celebrated work, *The Rise and Fall of Strategic Planning* (1993), hints at a similarly iconoclastic attitude towards strategy, a subject in which he is, in fact, an acknowledged master.

Rosabeth Moss Kanter

Kanter is a sociologist at heart and takes a humanistic approach to success in the new economy. Her best known works are *The Change Masters* (1983) and *Evolve!* (2001). You might find it useful to mention that she is far from being the first female management guru – that was efficiency pioneer Lillian Gilbreth (1878–1972).

Stephen Covey

Covey brings common sense to management theory. His success is attributed to the accessibility and the simplicity of the messages in his work.

He is best known for *The Seven Habits of Highly Effective People* (1989), which has sold over 25 million copies. This focuses on how to achieve 'centredness' and realise potential at the personal, leadership and corporate level. It demands that leaders commit to continual learning, espouse the culture of service orientation, lead a balanced life and also see life as an adventure. Not much to ask, really.

Nordström and Ridderstråle

Two Swedes, Kjell Nordström and his writing partner Jonas Ridderstråle, are unusual management gurus, and not just because of their shaven heads and black leather pants. Typical of the 61 slogans that they use is 'shopping and f***ing', the focus of which is on globalisation and innovation.

Their best-known work is *Funky Business* (1999) which breezes away the cobwebs of old management. For 'old' read anything that pre-dates them.

John Kotter

Kotter, not to be confused with Kotler, has been hailed as the best speaker in the world on topics of leadership and change. His key book is *Force for Change* (1990). His specialities are leadership, culture and managing change.

One might venture to suggest that being the best speaker doesn't necessarily guarantee literary fluency, but that might be pure jealousy on our part.

Laurence Peter

Peter's mainstream work concerned emotionally disturbed children so it should come as no surprise that he has made a big contribution to management theory. This is the Peter Principle which states that 'In a hierarchy, every employee tends to rise to his level of incompetence.' The corollary is that, in time, every post tends to be occupied by an employee who is incompetent to carry out its duties.

As a book, *The Peter Principle* (1969) may be a good example of a parallel principle, i.e., written work tends to be expanded to the point where it loses its impact and thus some, or all, of its merit. For example, a brilliant and pithy concept tends to be expanded into an article. A good article too often forms the basis for a book containing no new ideas of any value. A bestselling book becomes a series, all repeating the same thing. To be honest, most truly great ideas are better off staying as slogans. One of the best books anyone can read is a good book of quotations – to quote Sir Winston Churchill.

Advanced bluffers might find it useful to mention that although the theory is Peter's, the man who turned it into a book is Raymond Hull. So you can blame him.

Shepherd Mead

Not, strictly speaking, a true management theorist, Mead has to be included in *The Bluffer's Guide to Management* because of our sympathy for the sentiment behind the title of his seminal work, *How to Succeed in Business Without Really Trying*. The book included valuable insights into US management and was later turned into a memorable musical. Mead allows managers to have hobbies, for example, provided that they coincide with those of the company president. The hit songs that sprung from his insights include 'The Company Way' and 'I Believe in You', a touching love song sung by the hero to himself in the mirror, when he is given the key to the executive washroom.

You should be aware of a major elephant trap yawning in front of you in any reference to the name Shepherd Mead. It is uncomfortably similar to the name of Britain's oldest brewer, Shepherd Neame, and should you get the two of them confused it could lead to a lot of sniggering about where your real interests lie.

THE DEADLY SINS

Good management is not necessarily about flair or excellence. It may often be about getting things right more than 50% of the time, if only by avoiding the crass errors of your contemporaries. This, for the bluffer, must be particularly comforting. Note that it does not mean avoiding risk. Calculated risk is crucial to business growth. Avoidable stupidity is not.

Your motto should be: 'Accentuate the positive, eliminate the negative.' Management types love that sort of talk.

Should anyone ask, say you are quoting the philosopher Johnny Mercer; most people won't know that he was actually an American songwriter.

The secret of good management is avoiding bad management. Good managers don't:

- panic (well, not openly, anyway)
- abuse staff (as above)
- blame people (ditto)
- get aggressive
- pluck assumptions out of thin air

- fear change
- mistake action for thought
- fall hopelessly in love with the product
- stop learning
- talk more than they listen
- invoke 'necessity' as a reason for anything
- gossip (unless it's irresistibly juicy)
- go on holiday with the boss.

THE DEADLY SINS OF MANAGEMENT

The fact that we lump the following items under 'deadly' sins does not imply that these are the only management sins; as with proper sins, they are always inventing or discovering more. But here are a few of the things that managers do, and should not do.

Worry

Never worry. If this ideal sounds rather difficult in practice, just reflect for a moment. If there is something wrong, one of two courses is possible: either you can do something about it or you can't. If you can, do it. If you can't, you can't.

It is amazing how many problems solve themselves if you ignore them. Of the rest, most are soon reduced to manageable proportions when you analyse them and break them down into a number of relatively easy tasks. Failing that, give them to someone else to worry about.

Assuming the Worst

Relatively few people actively strive to do something

damaging or destructive. This may seem surprising, given the state of some organisations, but it is true.

So it is unwise to leap to conclusions about sabotage when there may only be a failure to communicate. Do not take radical action unless and until you are sure nothing less than radical action will do.

MSU

The Malady of Spurious Urgency afflicts most managers from time to time. In moments of crisis or plain ordinary pressure, there is a great temptation to allocate unreasonably high priorities to matters which in real terms are simply trivial or not really all that urgent. This is a close relation of the urge to be seen doing something in a crisis.

The acid test of the true manager under pressure is that he or she is the only one not immediately doing something. The real manager is thinking before acting – or at least appearing to think. You may very well be paralysed by uncertainty but if you can pass it off as keeping cool under pressure, it is better than running around doing the wrong thing for the sake of doing something.

Lateness

Those who are inefficient in little things are inefficient in big things, and repeated lateness is a telltale symptom of a bad manager. Worse, it is contagious. Weak bosses see their privilege of being late as a sign of power. They do not realise that employees take their lead from the boss and will see no reason not to be late themselves – so long as they are one minute less late than the boss.

Communicating Indirectly

Mistrust all second-hand communications. All other things being equal, you can guarantee that anyone conveying a message, no matter what their intentions, will in some way distort it. The classic case is one where all the good intentions run in the same direction. Consider the following module (as we say in management-speak):

On the first of the month, a manager tells his secretary to make sure a certain package is delivered to a client's home on the seventh, when the client returns from holiday. The secretary, with commendable initiative, decides to leave a margin of error and tells the despatch office to send it a bit early, so that it arrives on the fifth. The despatch office in turn shows initiative and leaves a further margin of error, sending it out immediately, so that it arrives on the third.

Thanks to these well-meaning people, the package is left on the client's doorstep for four days – and, of course, the manager neglected to mention to the secretary that its contents were perishable. This sort of thing happens all the time.

The moral of the story is to communicate directly and verify directly.

Murphy's Law

Management is no place for the easily discouraged. You have to be able to embrace the famous Murphy's Law: 'If something can go wrong, it will.'

To this universal truth can be added:

1. It is easier to get into something than to get out of it.

2. Nothing you do, however brilliantly conceived and executed, will ever satisfy more than 5% of the people concerned.

3. The legibility of a copy or email attachment is inversely proportional to its importance.

4. If you perceive that there are four possible ways in which a procedure can go wrong, and circumvent these, then a fifth way, unprepared for, will promptly develop. Two people can have a discussion, but a third will turn it into an argument.

5. Nothing that seems simple is.

6. Whenever you set out to do something, something else must be done first.

7. Take the worst-case scenario, then double it.

All make the same point, and it is not negativity but sound advice: 'Hope for the best, but be ready for the worst.'

FINALLY. TWO MANAGEMENT LESSONS

Lesson One
A crow sat on a tree doing nothing all day long. A rabbit saw the crow and asked: 'Can I sit like you and

do nothing all day long?' The crow answered: 'Certainly. Why not?' So the rabbit sat under the tree and did nothing all day long. Towards sunset, a fox appeared, jumped on the rabbit and ate it.

Management lesson: To be sitting and doing nothing you must be sitting very, very high up.

Lesson Two

A turkey was chatting with a bull. 'I would love to be able to get to the top of that tree,' sighed the turkey, 'but I haven't got the energy.'

'Well,' said the bull, 'my droppings are packed with nutrients, so why not try some?' The turkey ate a lump of dung and found it gave him enough strength to reach the lowest branch of the tree. The next day he ate some more and reached the second branch. By the fourth day he was proudly perched at the top of the tree. Then a farmer spotted him and shot him.

Management lesson: Bullshit might get you to the top, but it won't keep you there.

'To be sitting and doing nothing you must be sitting very, very high up.'

There's no point in pretending that you know everything about management – nobody does – but if you've got this far and you've absorbed at least a modicum of the information and advice contained within these pages, then you will almost certainly know more than 99% of what the rest of the human race does about what it involves, how it is mostly made up as you go along, how far you can get without any formal training, and why – on the whole – whether we like it or not, the world will always be divided into managers and the managed.

What you now do with this information is up to you, but here's a suggestion: be confident about your newfound knowledge, see how far it takes you, but above all have fun using it. You are now a bona fide expert in the art of bluffing about how to convince people that you actually know what you're doing in the workplace. And always remember: if in doubt, delegate.

JARGON AND GLOSSARY

Jargon appears to be the major barrier to the understanding of almost any commercial or industrial activity and most management functions. It would be mischievous to imply that the resulting obfuscation is deliberate, but the net effect is the same as if it was.

To be fair, the intention of the originator of each new buzzword was probably to clarify, but there are just so many of them, and everyone seems to use the same expressions to mean different things.

Part of the fun in talking business jargon is inventing it on the hoof and watching clients and colleagues nod sagely as they struggle to make any sense of what you're talking about. Any phrase involving the words 'matrix', 'interface' or 'paradigm' usually does the trick.

For further evidence of how quickly the language of business and management is evolving and/or degenerating, turn to any reference within these pages to 'digital strategy'. Bluffers don't have to be completely fluent in digi-speak to get by, but it's useful to have at least a handful of incomprehensible hogwash up your sleeve to give the definite impression that you're in tune with the digital zeitgeist.

And if all else fails, then just make it up (as above). You're a bluffer, after all.

Action A noun commonly used as a verb (as in 'let's action that'), intended to convey a dynamic course of conduct, more in hope than expectation.

Aspirational content. Too clever and too expensive.

Ballpark figure An estimate 'in the area of'; derived from US baseball stadia, which actually cover a very wide area.

Bandwidth The maximum amount of something that can be squeezed out of limited resources of money, time or expertise to accommodate an impossible request (otherwise known as 'stretching capacity').

Best practice What every organisation claims to offer – in other words, standard practice.

Blue-sky thinking Fantasising.

Brainstorming In theory, innovation multiplied by the number of participants; in practice, innovation divided by the number of participants.

Budgeting Imposing a set of financial rules and restrictions, within a framework of predictions, which are invariably ignored.

Buzzword bingo Also known as 'Bullshit' bingo, this is a high-risk game invented to make meetings more interesting. Players are covertly equipped with cards with 'buzz' words and expressions, and tick them off whenever they are used. Those chairing the meeting rarely see the funny side when the winner shouts 'Bingo!'

Cascade. Best used as a verb (no, really). To cascade. With the hissily insistent subject line diktat 'Please cascade this to all departments', corporate group emails have become a veritable Niagara of crucial information delegation.

Caution-orientation The sensible but ultimately unprofitable practice of taking absolutely no risk whatsoever.

Change catalyst Something that instigates a different course of action – usually the realisation that the last one didn't work.

Churn rate. Nothing to do with dairy farming. It's when sensitive CEOs blub on being told that fewer people in Q2 than in Q1 are subscribing to their companies' world-beating services, and as a result some underlings are going to have to be restructured.

Competitive advantage A superiority in products or services that every business claims to have over every other business; usually wishful thinking.

Conversion. The online equivalent of a full-immersion baptism among grateful digital evangelists. Also means, happily, that the 'converted' user-turned-customer will have parted with their debit and credit card details.

Core competency Wasted potential.

Create shockwaves. Finish building a website.

Customer-focused The realisation that if you don't give customers what they want, they tend to go away.

Cutting edge Essentially meaningless words but modern syntax demands that they are always inserted before the words 'technology' and 'technique'.

Delegation Passing the buck.

Digital strategy meeting. Also known as 'is it lunchtime yet?'

Disruptive. No digital content is worth its weight in multi-platform, fully responsive optimisation unless it behaves like an unruly schoolkid on the brink of exclusion.

Dwell time. Sometimes called loitering. The challenge for digital strategists is to work out whether the loiterer is hanging out on a web page with intent to do something; intent to buy, to share, to convert, to wake up, to switch off, or to call the authorities.

Empowerment Passing the buck to somebody who isn't expecting it.

Flowcharts An effective method of showing simple activities in an unnecessarily complex way.

Future-proof Taking action to minimise possible negative consequences by applying a 'caution-orientated' 'ring fence' (*see* above and below) to a particular course of action which is yet to take place. It usually involves finding a suitable scapegoat for when it goes horribly wrong.

Game-changer. Expensive redesign by over-priced and overrated London digital agency.

Game plan Trendy name for strategy but without calling it a strategy, so it can be dropped more easily when it fails.

Goalpost rules As in 'moving the...', i.e., changing the rules of the game when you're halfway through it. (That's if you were bothering to observe them in the first place.)

Headspace As in 'give it some...', a stated intention to think about something...later.

Infographics. Clever diagrams that teenagers know how to do for breaking up large dreary lumps of text.

Interface An interaction between two separate entities which can be people, concepts or material objects;

'joining up' or 'connection' mean much the same thing but don't sound nearly as impressive.

Kevlar it Testing the strength of an idea by chucking everything at it, then realising it needs to be wrapped in much stronger material before it stands up.

Knowledge bank Affectionate nickname for the resident know-it-all in a team; Google is usually more effective and a lot less expensive.

Knowledge management Concept whereby an enterprise 'consciously and comprehensively gathers, organises, shares and analyses its internal knowledge' in terms of systems, resources and people skills; basically what managers thought they were doing already, before anyone coined the term.

Mental mainframe The collective cerebral resources of a team or organisation; usually where brainstorming takes place (*see* above).

Mentoring Training with delusions of grandeur.

Metrics Standards of measurement, popular with digital types. Mention 'metrics' in a meeting, and you'll elicit a hallowed hush and narrowing of eyes of the assembled disciples, as they switch into serious mode. Try it. It's fun.

Mindset Set of assumptions, methods, prejudices or

delusions which are so set in concrete that there isn't much point in trying to change them.

Mission-focused A stated intention to remain absolutely and unswervingly committed to a particular objective or course of action; the mindset (*see* above) of a kamikaze pilot.

Park To do that thing we were talking about which no one really understood – and which someone made a pig's ear of explaining in the meeting – next year. Possibly.

People-based management Just made this one up; feel free to use it for something/anything.

Performance-based Concept that involves rewarding people according to their abilities and results; a concept of justice that is unlikely to be realised this side of the afterlife.

Principle-centred Generally used in the context of leadership, a term expressing a profound intention to use best practice (*see* above) to ensure the most exalted ethical standards and commitment to professional integrity; strictly for public relations use only.

Prioritising Means of ensuring that the least-pressing matters are attended to first.

Production matrix An environment where a thing is nurtured, developed and very occasionally produced;

otherwise known as an R&D department (as in Resist and Delay).

Project percolator As in 'popping in the...', an expression for putting a plan of action permanently on hold; also a euphemism for a chronic inability to get the simplest task done.

Pushing the envelope Much-loved aviation term for taking an aircraft beyond the limits of what it was designed to do, and then pushing it further. In a business context, this might involve pursuing new markets or business plans and then watching them spectacularly explode.

Putting it to bed To complete a task after considerable time and effort, and hope it will quietly go to sleep.

Reach out To ask in a caring sharing kind of way.

Results-driven A way of stressing the importance of accountability and continuous improvement; wishful thinking.

Revert. Ignore.

Rightsize to A more positive way of saying 'downsize', which is itself a more positive way of saying 'make people redundant'.

Ring-fence The practice of isolating a course of action

or designated pot of money from outside risk; usually a sign of corporate politics at work.

Rollout The expansion of campaigns from a single test market; 'rollback' is the opposite, a strategic retreat to work out what went wrong.

Scuba it Expression for diving in at the deep end of an area of zero knowledge, crossing everything and hoping for the best.

Search engine optimisation. *The* thing. The first, the last, the everything (apologies to Barry White). Online alchemy, the gold-rush; clever but simple, semi-mystical shining path to digital content glory.

Shifting paradigm A pattern of behaviour that is acting erratically; the expression could apply to anything from senior management after a long lunch, to junior management not demanding regular salary reviews.

Silo A place anyone works in, but not for thinking. It's not good to think in silos. Silos are bad.

Soft launch. Don't tell anyone about the new website, as they're bound to hate it and then laugh at it with all their friends

Strategic gap A gaping hole in the heart of a plan of action; usually junior management's fault.

Strategic staircasing. A business plan. No stairs necessary. There is no staircase. It's a business bungalow.

Strategic visioning Thinking about a strategy for planning and decision-making, otherwise known as 'planning to make plans'.

Synergy The idea that the combination of two forces will create an effect that is greater than the sum of individual forces; also known as the '2 + 2 = 5 effect'; the fact that this is a mathematical impossibility is usually ignored.

Think outside the box To come up with hare-brained and totally unworkable ideas.

Think tank A forum where people 'think outside the box', thus coming up with even more deranged ideas and reckless possible future courses of action which have to have the box lid kept firmly on them.

Thought exchange. Discussion.

Thought leadership Unusual concept that involves a team leader actually thinking something through before proposing its implementation; a dangerous precedent.

Thought shower. Brainstorming's leaner fitter cousin. Unisex, and very inclusive, and best held in an office with a whiteboard and colourful marker pens, rather than in communal changing rooms at the gym.

Transformative. A website that works, whereas the previous one didn't.

User experience. Sitting in front of a screen, reading stuff.

Webinar. Remote video meeting/presentation, all done virtually over a computer where the disassembled throng could be anywhere from Dawlish to Dar es Salaam. Some might even be in the kitchen.

Wingwalking Never let go of what you're holding on to until you've got hold of something else. Like a job.

Wish-list. Too clever and too expensive.

BLUFFER'S NOTES